TI
ALCOHOL, AGGRESSION AND ADOLESCENCE

TITLES IN THE FACTS ABOUT . . . SERIES

J. S. Baxter *Child Witnesses*

J. B. Davies and N. Coggans *Adolescent Drug Abuse*

N. Coggans and S. McKellar *Alcohol, Aggression and Adolescence*

B. Gillham *Child Physical Abuse*

B. Gillham *Child Sexual Abuse*

J. A. Thomson *Child Pedestrian Accidents*

THE FACTS ABOUT

ALCOHOL, AGGRESSION

AND ADOLESCENCE

NIALL COGGANS AND SUSAN MCKELLAR

CASSELL

Cassell
Wellington House
125 Strand
London WC2R 0BB

215 Park Avenue South
New York
NY 10003

First published 1995

British Library Cataloguing-in-Publication Data
A catalogue record for this book is available from the British Library.

ISBN 0-304-32664-X (hardback)
0-304-32666-6 (paperback)

Typeset by York House Typographic Ltd
Printed and bound in Great Britain by Mackays of Chatham PLC, Chatham, Kent

CONTENTS

SERIES FOREWORD

The idea for this series came from an awareness that much of the media hype, and some of the professional practice, relating to major social problems involving children and adolescents was singularly ill-informed. At the same time there was a notable lack of short, accessible summaries of the relevant research data by which people could inform themselves.

Not surprisingly, the conclusions that are drawn from a careful consideration of the evidence challenge many generally held assumptions – at all levels of popular and professional concern.

Bill Gillham

ACKNOWLEDGEMENTS

The authors are grateful to the funding bodies whose support made possible much of the work which is included in this book. In particular we are grateful to the Alcohol Education and Research Council for funding experimental research into alcohol and aggression; and to The Portman Group for funding research into the wider context of health promotion in schools, from which the work on the influence of peers is derived. We are also grateful to the editor of *Drugs: Education, Prevention and Policy*, published by Carfax, for permission to utilize the material which forms the basis for Chapter 5, which was published in that journal in 1994.

THE AUTHORS

Niall Coggans is a Senior Lecturer in the Department of Pharmaceutical Sciences, University of Strathclyde, Glasgow. Susan McKellar is a Research Fellow now working in the Department of Human Nutrition, University of Glasgow. Between them the authors have extensive research experience of alcohol and drug problems, alcohol and drug education, alcohol-related disorder and aggression, and various other aspects of health education and health promotion.

1

WHAT IS THE PROBLEM?

INTRODUCTION

Alcohol-related disorder, whether hooliganism, aggression or violence, seems to be both a perennial and a worsening problem. It appears that in today's world young people regularly get drunk, fight amongst themselves, and harass or attack others. Moreover, such incidents have been reported in big cities, where you might expect such behaviour, in small towns, and even in rural areas. In the late 1980s concern was expressed by the Association of Chief Police Officers that such disorder was widespread, and causing disruption in communities that only ten years previously had been havens of rural tranquillity (Tuck, 1989).

This book goes beyond the dramatic and not always accurate media accounts of the problem. That a problem exists is not in doubt, but what exactly do we mean when we talk about alcohol-related aggression and violence? Is it a new phenomenon? Why do young people drink and/or get into trouble? What harm does alcohol do to the health of young people whether they get into bother or not? Is there a link between alcohol and other, illegal, drugs? And what can be done to tackle the problem at a personal level and at an organizational level?

The purpose here is to look at some of the key issues surrounding alcohol and aggression with particular reference to adolescence. After introducing some of the issues, there is some examination of the available statistics, with reference to prevalence of violence and offending, as well as patterns of drinking, and how young people differ from older age groups, where the data permit. A central theme of the book is the way in which young people develop attitudes and behaviours that can be defined as problematic in relation to alcohol and aggression. This involves appraisal of the relationship between alcohol and aggression, re-appraisal of the widely held view that young people are led astray by others – so-called peer pressure – and some discussion of the choices available to people who have to cope with aggression. The importance of social and cultural influences is explored and the issue of intervention is raised. In some respects the reader will be reassured that the problem is not as widespread as might have been thought, but there are other aspects of the problem that are more intractable. The role of education in preventing alcohol-related problems seems assured, for example, but the efficacy of the many initiatives in this area is not quite so certain. It is not the intention here to reprise some of the problems of efficacy of alcohol and drug education. This issue is explored in detail elsewhere (Coggans *et al.*, 1991a and 1991b). Nonetheless, the problem of low effectiveness of educational interventions is recognized, though there are some indications that some groups of offenders respond positively to certain forms of alcohol education (Baldwin, 1993). Drawing on the latest research evidence with a minimum of psychological or sociological jargon, there is something for everybody in this book, from professionals working in the field to the more casual reader.

YOUNG PEOPLE AND ALCOHOL

Received wisdom holds that alcohol and violence go together, that people are more likely to be aggressive under the influence of alcohol. It is also widely accepted that young people, being less accustomed to the effects of alcohol, are less likely to control their behaviour under its influence. However, the problem of adolescent drinking and violence cannot be seen as somehow a separate problem from the wider issue of alcohol and aggression in the general population, or as separate from the problem of teenage delinquency in general. After all, much of the motivation for young people to drink alcohol is that it is seen as adult, sophisticated, or even 'manly'. Many studies over the years have drawn the conclusion that alcohol is *related* to aggression and violence, from assault to rape or even murder. Some studies which have examined the effects of alcohol under scientifically controlled conditions have also supported the conclusion that alcohol does indeed make it more likely that people will behave aggressively towards others. In addition, there is also evidence reported in the literature that alcohol influences aggression more than it affects other types of behaviour (Bushman and Cooper, 1990). However, as will be discussed in more detail later, such studies require careful interpretation before attributing too great a role to alcohol in the genesis of aggression. While there may be cause for concern about the effects of alcohol on young people, where aggression or hooliganism is concerned, there are good reasons to be cautious about over-simplistic assumptions concerning the effects of alcohol on aggressive behaviour, without taking other factors such as personal history and social context into account.

Despite the apparently high level of alcohol-related disorder involving young people in recent years there is nothing new about the phenomenon. In fact the problem of alcohol-related hooliganism has been with us for centuries. Moreover, we must recognize the central role that alcohol consumption plays in the lives of young people, as well as in the lives of the population at large. Evidence supports the view that alcohol misuse is a significant problem among some young people. However, it must also be recognized that the extent of the problem is not as great as it is sometimes perceived to be. There appears to be something of a recurring pattern of moral panic about media treatment of alcohol misuse and associated behaviour amongst young people (Dorn, 1983; May, 1992). While there is a great deal of concern about the problem of drinking and disorder, the fact remains that drinking in itself is essentially a *normal* activity for young people. That this is the case not only in major cities was revealed by a recent survey, undertaken as part of an investigation into the phenomenon of alcohol-related violence in non-metropolitan areas, which confirmed the importance of going to the pub for young people. Drinking, particularly weekend drinking, is a regular pastime for young people, especially young males (Tuck, 1989). However, only a minority of these young people reported drinking heavily. Which reminds us that while alcohol is central to the lives of many young people, it is largely a normal activity both in the sense of its being something that most young people do to some extent, and in the sense of its being something they do with complications arising for some but not most young people.

Alcohol consumption among the general population increased during the post-war years with consumption in 1984 running at twice the level of 1950, according to a report from the Royal College of General Practitioners in 1986, although it is best to be cautious about changes in consumption patterns over relatively short time periods. For example, it is also possible to point to times in the more distant past when alcohol consumption was higher with endemic drunkenness, such as during the latter half of the nineteenth century. The present licensing regulations have their origins in the need to introduce controls on availability during the First World War when the debilitating effects of alcohol were thought to be seriously detracting from the war effort. In more recent years, however, consumption of alcohol in real terms appears not to have risen (Thomas *et al.*, 1994).

To some extent the general increase in consumption indicated in the post-war years seems to be reflected in drinking patterns among younger people too. The Royal College of Psychiatrists commented a few years ago, in their report *Alcohol: Our Favourite Drug* (1986), that there were worrying signs of drink-related problems amongst younger people, including medical problems and convictions for drunkenness. Moreover, 18- to 24-year-olds are often the heaviest drinkers (Royal College of General Practitioners, 1986). However, there is little or no good data on younger age groups which would permit an assessment of trends or difference over decades.

Nonetheless, most young people drink moderately and the pattern of reported consumption among young people has not changed over the last decade. Indeed, most young people develop patterns of drinking behaviour that are *not* problematic (Sharpe and Lowe, 1989).

By the age of 10–14 years most young people have had some experience of alcohol, usually in the home in the presence of parents or other older relatives. The home background plays a very important part in the way in which young people learn their early drinking practices, and it is often asserted that the best place for young people to experience alcohol is the home; the assumption being that if first and early experience of alcohol is in the home, under the supervision of parents, then young people are more likely to develop moderate alcohol consumption habits. This will only hold true, in the main, for those children whose parents' alcohol-related behaviour is moderate and whose alcohol-related attitudes are consistent with the messages they want their children to adhere to.

The home can therefore be the context for the transmission of alcohol-related behaviour that is broadly in line with that of the parents. Which means that on the one hand the home can be an important influence on the establishment of sensible drinking and sensible attitudes to alcohol; on the other hand, the home can be an important influence on the development of harmful drinking patterns and attitudes towards alcohol that could be problematic.

Given the importance of the home in the development of drinking practices the question arises of how important is the social or cultural transmission of alcohol- and aggression-related attitudes and behaviour? The nature–nurture debate is an old and a continuing one with only one certainty; namely, that the way any human behaves cannot be the result of either genetic or cultural influence alone. There is no doubt that culture plays an extremely important role in the development of social or anti-social behaviour. But it is the extent to which young people are exposed to a particular cultural influence that matters, not whether a cultural influence is only fleetingly present. For example, it is unlikely that exposure to a violent film on one occasion only will necessarily have a permanent and deleterious effect on that young person. The recent publicity surrounding young criminals and their exposure to 'video nasties' has generally overlooked the (high?) probability that such young people grow up in an environment characterized by aggressiveness. This aggressiveness might originate with one significant other such as a parent, or it could be more pervasive and be a defining characteristic of the family 'micro-culture'. More worrying still is the possibility that young people become part of a wider 'macro-culture' in which social interactions within their community are mostly typified by aggression and violence.

Much has been made in recent years about the ethos of schools and the importance of this intangible aspect of school life in the development of academically competent and socially skilled young adults. Drawing on its Greek origins, the word *ethos* (nature or disposition) is used to describe the prevailing characteristics and attitudes of a community or system. The usefulness of the term in the present context is to widen out the nurture side of the debate from a narrow focus on a young person's relationships with parents and siblings to encompass the wider social influences of all those within the orbit of a given young person. If we can talk in terms of the ethos of the micro-culture (proximal or immediate social influences) and the ethos of the macro-culture (distal or wider social influences) then we can see how both micro- and macro-culture might interact to encourage certain attitudes and certain forms of behaviour. Thus, if the ethos both of the micro-culture and of the macro-culture is aggressive or places high value on abusive forms of alcohol intake there is less to counter the development of anti-social behaviour than would be the case where the child is growing up in an anti-social micro-culture but with a wider macro-culture which is antipathetic towards aggressiveness and abusive forms of intoxication. The distinction between proximal and distal cultural influences is useful as a way of identifying different sources of socio-cultural influences on young people. Moreover, to talk in terms of consonant and dissonant cultural ethos helps as a reminder that in any one individual case there is a whole package of influences to take into account when deciding whether to blame, say, exposure to violent films and videos or the attitudes and behaviour of significant others. Just as a slap from a parent will not necessarily result in an aggressive and violent young adult if this is an unusual act which runs counter to the ethos of the child's micro-culture, infrequent exposure to violent film or video material will not give rise to an aggressive adult if this cultural input is uncharacteristic and is countered by the normal ethos of a social environment which places high value on positive and non-aggressive social interactions (Hamburg, 1992).

As will be demonstrated in Chapter 4, the social context surrounding an aggressive encounter has a crucial role in determining the level of aggression presented. Where specific instances of cultural input take place within a social context that reinforces such values and attitudes there is a greater likelihood that the young person will also come to place greater value on anti-social ways. In other words, the ethos of both micro-culture and macro-culture plays an important part in the origins and perpetuation of aggressiveness, other anti-social behaviour, and abusive patterns of drinking.

It is worth noting that most parents accept that their children will drink alcohol and seem to be happy that they do so, providing that they do so sensibly. Moreover, what is termed under-age drinking (that is, under 18 years of age, the minimum legal age for purchasing alcohol from licensed premises in Britain) is so widespread that it can only be considered deviant in relation to the law, not in relation to what is normal behaviour amongst teenagers.

Once young people reach the age of about 15 years their involvement with and experience of alcohol tends to take place outside the home. Prior to reaching the stage of drinking alcohol in the public domain, i.e., drinking in pubs or elsewhere away from the scrutiny of adults, alcohol-related behaviour and attitudes tend to reflect the drinking behaviour and attitudes of their parents. After the move towards drinking with friends outside parental view the amount and frequency of consumption, as well as attitudes to alcohol, take on a more adult style. That is, drinking goes up and attitudes to alcohol tend to reflect wider adult attitudes to drinking. This manifests itself in such things as seeing drinking as an essential part of the transition to adulthood. Thus, it becomes accepted, if not desirable, for many young people that they will drink to intoxication and some will engage in the sorts of disorderly behaviour associated with intoxication. The extent to which young people start to misuse alcohol and behave in an unruly manner probably reflects the home background, the wider social context, and the alcohol-related behaviour and attitudes of the friends with whom young people are mixing. Another factor which has been thought to play a part in the development of harmful patterns of drinking is the 'personality' of the drinker. This factor and the over-willingness to explain problem behaviour in terms of peer pressure will be discussed in more detail in later chapters. For now let it suffice to say that the development of drinking patterns in any individual will be a complex interaction of these various influences.

ANTI-SOCIAL BEHAVIOUR AND OFFENDING

When considering the problems of disorder and intoxication among young people it is important to be aware of the wider context of the prevalence of delinquency and offending. Moreover, there are different levels of seriousness and different categories of problem behaviour evident among young people. Adolescence is a time during which it has been noted there is a markedly high prevalence of anti-social behaviour and commission of offences. Anti-social behaviour is a rather vague category of behaviour which has no clear definition in law. Some acts will be deemed to be anti-social with a high degree of consensus, such as burglary and violence, while others will be deemed anti-social only by a minority, such as swearing and raucous behaviour. Offending on the other hand has a clearer definition within the legal framework: namely, an act which in terms of the age of the perpetrator and the criminal law is 'capable of being followed by criminal proceedings' (McMurran and Hollin, 1993). In addition, within the context of offending there are acts which are offences by virtue of the age of the person (i.e., they are not old enough to do something) and those acts which are offences irrespective of the age of the person.

Estimates of actual offending across the range of all offences vary, but there is agreement that the actual proportion of young people who commit offences is higher than official records show. Bearing in mind that most offences committed by adolescents are minor in importance and largely related to their age, it has been estimated that if unre--

corded offences were to be aggregated with official statistics most if not all young people would be included in the category of young offenders (Farrington, 1987); although there would be problems of compatibility of data sets in terms of official records and self-reports having different data characteristics. The essential point is that the adolescent years are a time when offending and anti-social behaviour reaches a lifetime peak. However, this is largely accounted for by the numbers of young people engaging in problem behaviour rather than the incidence per individual rising dramatically, although some young people do become more seriously involved. This, however, is not the same as saying that all adolescents are somehow similar in their potential for future criminality. American research underlines this point, revealing that more young people commit offences, particularly around 16–17 years of age, while the average rate of offence per individual remains fairly constant (Wolfgang *et al.*, 1987).

While the high prevalence of offending in adolescence is accounted for by more young people misbehaving, there are also discernible characteristics related to future persistent criminality to be found in the teenage years. For example, a number of factors can be described as risk factors, though they should not be seen as necessarily causal as the data are associational, including poor parenting and early behavioural problems, low income, low IQ, and parental criminality (West, 1982). Recidivism is higher among young offenders with six or more convictions and among those who are convicted at an early age (Farrington, 1983). The precise ways in which the characteristics identified by West (1982) operate as risk factors are difficult to define, being neither necessary nor sufficient for the creation of young criminals.

Does prison work?

A recent Home Office report showed that reconviction rates among former prisoners are extremely high. Particularly dramatic is the fact that 71% of offenders under 21 are convicted of another criminal offence within two years of release from detention, climbing to 82% after four years.

92% of 15–16 year olds who serve time in youth custody centres are reconvicted within two years.

(Home Office report cited in the *Guardian*, 24 June 1994)

Violence against the person

Official statistics on offences of alcohol-related violence are difficult to interpret because of the ways in which offences are recorded. For example, offences of drunkenness, including aggravated drunkenness, and offences of violence are recorded separately. Moreover, age breakdowns are coarse-grained in some instances, though finer-grain breakdowns are available in others. In the case of offences of violence against the person, Home Office data from 1992 for England and Wales show that of a grand total of 67,000 offences committed by males and females, defined as guilty or cautioned, the proportion attributable to males was 85.5 per cent while that for females was 14.5 per cent (Home Office, 1993a).

Available breakdowns by age indicate that, as a proportion of offences of violence against the person committed by males, those under 21 years of age were responsible for 37.3 per cent while males 21 years of age and over were responsible for 62.7 per cent. In the same vein, the proportion of all female offences of violence against the person perpetrated by under-21s was 51.5 per cent with the over-21s responsible for 48.5 per cent.

Further breakdowns on the under-21s reveal that the offences of violence committed by young males 10–13 years of age, 14–16 years of age, and 17–20 years of age were 3.3 per cent, 12.6 per cent, and 21.3 per cent respectively, as a proportion of the total of offences of violence against the person perpetrated by all males. Similarly for females under 21 those committed by young females 10–13 years of age, 14–16 years of age, and 17–20 years of age were 6.2 per cent, 26.8 per cent, and 18.6 per cent respectively, as a proportion of the total of offences of violence against the person recorded carried out by all females.

The first and most obvious conclusion drawn from these data is that males are responsible for most recorded violence. In terms of the trends discernible it appears that male violent offenders are more prevalent in the 17–20 age group, while female offenders appear to peak at 14–16 years of age. However, the rate at which the trend drops after 21 years, i.e., over the remainder of the age range, is not clear from these data. The proportion of offences of violence against the person carried out in 1992 by females in all age groups under 21 years, and by males under 16 years, showed a slight increase over the 1991 figures. These increases may not be significant in a statistical sense and the safest inference is that the proportion of such offences which can be attributed to the youngest age groups is not diminishing and may even be on the increase.

Turning to offences of drunkenness and aggravated drunkenness (i.e., all offences of drunkenness other than simple drunkenness) data for 1991 reveal that young people under 18 years of age represented 3 per cent of the total set of those found guilty or cautioned. Those aged 18–20 years represented 12 per cent, 21–29 years of age 34 per cent, and 30–59 years of age 47 per cent. It was also noted that the peak ages for offences of drunkenness were 20 years of age for males and 19 years for females (Home Office, 1993b).

It appears from these data that the concern with young people being responsible for a significant proportion of violent offences and for drunkenness is reflected to some extent in official statistics. However, these figures are presented here more to obtain a broad-brush picture of how such offences, that come to the notice of the law *and* are progressed to the point of conviction or caution, break down in terms of age. It is a truism to assert that these figures do not reflect the actual state of affairs. Moreover, the actual state of affairs is further complicated, within the terms of this book, inasmuch that the issue of alcohol, aggression and adolescence is relatively broad. That is, there is concern that alcohol-related disorder is a growing problem and a problem of young people. Yet, for every recorded offence of violence, or of drunkenness, there is a larger number of incidents including anti-social acts which will trouble people.

SEX DIFFERENCES

Men seem to be more aggressive than women. More men than women, for example, are involved in crimes of violence such as assault, actual and grievous bodily harm, and murder (Wilson and Herrnstein, 1985), a pattern that is more or less global. Men do appear to be more aggressive than women, both in terms of self-description and in terms of their potential for involvement in aggressive encounters (Reinisch and Sanders, 1986). While there is a consensus that men are more physically aggressive than women, a number of factors influence sex differences in aggression to the extent that caution is advised in assuming that sex differences are uniform under different conditions (Geen, 1990). For example, attitudes to stereotyped sex-role behaviours and the presence of same-sex role models can confound the expected pattern.

There is some debate about the underlying reasons for greater male aggressiveness. A number of reviews of the literature have informed this debate in recent years, with some difference in the conclusions drawn. For example, Maccoby and Jacklin (1974 and 1980) have argued that inheritance plays a significant role, basing their conclusions on cross-cultural similarity in greater male aggressiveness, the early appearance of greater male aggressiveness in the pre-school years, and some evidence that aggression can be influenced by sex hormones. Others have challenged these conclusions, suggesting that the extent of difference in aggressiveness between the sexes is less marked than that put forward by Maccoby and Jacklin. Moreover, it appears that sex differences decrease with age (Hyde, 1984; Eagly and Steffen, 1986).

It has been suggested that a key difference between men and women is their preferred mode of aggression, such that men and women only differ in terms of physical aggression but not with verbal aggression. Thus, men tended to be more aggressive in studies involving physical forms of aggression, with much less difference in studies involving verbal or psychological aggression (Eagly and Steffen, 1986). However, the role of contextual factors and lowered guilt can give rise to women being as aggressive as men (Larsen *et al.*, 1972). The power of cultural influences is also subject to some dispute. Eagly and Steffen argue that sex-related stereotyped social roles account for much of the difference between men and women, while Maccoby and Jacklin contend that inheritance is a significant factor that establishes basic sex differences.

It would appear that given the right circumstances and motivation women are capable of aggression and violence. While the relative contribution of inheritance and socio-cultural factors in aggression and violence is difficult to pin down exactly, it is more important to address the issue of ameliorating whatever contribution social and cultural influences make to the incidence of aggression. That there is a genetic basis upon which social and cultural influences will build in the shaping of aggressiveness is hardly in doubt. This is only part of the story and the remaining contribution of social and cultural factors is by definition malleable. The issue is to tackle what can be changed and that requires an emphasis on these factors.

CHAPTER SUMMARY

In this introductory chapter we have looked at some of the common beliefs and misapprehensions surrounding the tendency of young people to drink alcohol and become involved in violence. The degree to which drinking is seen as normal by all age groups and by young people in particular was discussed and we examined a range of factors, including the influence of both the immediate and the wider social context, which interact to create patterns of drinking and aggressive behaviour.

The incidence among young people of anti-social behaviour such as offences of drunkenness and of violence against the person was also discussed, and possible reasons for the sex differences to be found in such statistics were examined. These and other areas will be explored further in the following chapters.

2

DRINKING PATTERNS

HOW MUCH DO YOUNG PEOPLE DRINK?

Although there have been many local studies of the drinking behaviour of young people, the survey carried out by Marsh and colleagues for the Department of Health and Social Security in 1984 was the first *national* examination of drinking practices in adolescents between the ages of 13 and 17 (Marsh *et al.*, 1986). The General Household Survey carried out annually by the Office of Population Censuses and Surveys (OPCS) has included questions on drinking every two years since 1978, but these were confined to people over 18 until Marsh *et al.*'s Adolescent Drinking Survey revealed the extent of drinking in 16- and 17-year-olds. As a consequence, data on the drinking behaviour of this age group were obtained by OPCS in 1987, 1988, 1989, 1990 and 1992.

Methodological issues

Most researchers of drinking behaviour have emphasized the problems involved in obtaining reliable information. The main difficulties are generally considered to be under-reporting and faulty recall of the amount of alcohol consumed, and this would probably apply equally to adults or children. Under-reporting seems mainly to be unintentional, but it may sometimes occur deliberately because there is a family member nearby; for example in Marsh *et al.*'s (1986) survey Scottish 16-year-olds, who were interviewed at home, reported drinking less than the 14-year-olds seen at school. Incidents of over-reporting also seem to occur among adolescents, and Marsh *et al.* report having rejected data provided by a few subjects who claimed to have drunk lethal amounts of alcohol. In the same sample, examples of possible over-reporting such as the 6 boys in Scotland under 15 years of age who each claimed to have consumed over 20 units of alcohol on the previous Saturday night were not excluded, since these would probably be balanced by under-reporting.

In addition to the possibility of the young person's responses to a questionnaire being affected by the proximity of family, there are other ways in which the context may exert an influence on the information provided and these factors should also be taken into account. One such is the interviewer effect which has been shown in studies such as those carried out by Belson *et al.* (1968) and Davies and Baker (1987) where the manner in which the interview is conducted or the way in which the interviewer presents himself can make a significant difference to the information obtained. This effect was also demonstrated in an evaluation of drug education in Scotland (Coggans *et al.*, 1991b). A test of the reliability of the data was carried out in which school pupils were asked on two separate occasions to provide the same information on their drug and alcohol use, among other things. The pupils were led to believe that they were being questioned as part of two quite separate studies. On one occasion the data were obtained by a suit-wearing 'respectable' researcher while on the other occasion the researcher was informally dressed, acted casually and appeared relaxed about under-age drinking, illegal drug use and so on. Comparison of the two sets of data showed that the mean alcohol consumption reported to the 'casual' researcher was significantly higher than that reported to his 'respectable' counterpart. A further difficulty encountered when trying to estimate amounts of drink consumed at home where standard measures do not apply has led some researchers such as Hawker (1978) and McKechnie *et al.* (1977) to believe that only *frequency* of consumption, rather than quantity, can be measured.

Because of the acknowledged difficulties in obtaining accurate data, there has been some debate about which instruments are most appropriate for the investigation of drinking behaviour. The use of self-completion questionnaires has sometimes been criticized; for example, Plant *et al.* (1985) included a 'cautionary message' about surveys which use self-reports, suggesting that these are 'almost certainly only a rough guide' to behaviour. However, the use of self-completion questionnaires somewhat reduces the potential for interviewer bias, described above, and the practicability of this method is undeniable; such questionnaires have been employed by researchers such as Marsh *et al.* (1986), Hawker (1978), Stacey and Davies (1970) and Hartford and Spiegler (1983), as well as by Plant *et al.* (1985). As a way of attempting to overcome problems of faulty recall, some surveys have used a seven-day drinking diary in which drinkers enter their alcohol consumption for each day of the preceding week, starting with the previous day and working backwards. This method, used by Marsh and colleagues in their 1984 survey of adolescent drinking (Marsh *et al.*, 1986) and in the *ad hoc* OPCS surveys of drinking, is widely believed to stand the best chance of eliciting accurate information.

An alcohol-diary approach was not used in the General Household Survey as this method was considered too time-consuming given the range of topics which were to be covered. Instead, the General Household Survey asks respondents how often they have drunk each of five different types of alcoholic drink in the previous year and how much of each they usually consumed on any one occasion. These self-reports are then converted into standard units of alcohol and used to estimate average weekly consumption. The authors emphasize that this is not intended to represent a precise measure since the figures given by irregular drinkers for consumption on a 'usual' occasion cannot really be extrapolated to produce accurate weekly amounts. Nevertheless, the mean estimates of weekly consumption thus arrived at are used to compare groups, and these estimates tend to be higher than those obtained in the *ad hoc* OPCS surveys where alcohol diaries are used. In a period when Brewers' Society statistics indicate that the consumption of alcohol in real terms is not rising, it is probable that these higher figures result from the method of measurement.

While it is clearly important to keep the inherent methodological difficulties in mind when looking at the information obtained in the various surveys, it is also worth bearing in mind that comparisons between different studies have observed that the results tend to be broadly similar.

Early experience of alcohol

A study of alcohol and drug use in Scottish 13- to 16-year-olds published in 1991 indicated that three-quarters had experience of alcohol and nearly 10 per cent claimed to drink every week (Coggans *et al.*, 1991a). The survey of adolescent drinking carried out in 1984 by Marsh and colleagues found that 82 per cent of boys and 77 per cent of girls in England and Wales reported having had a 'proper drink' by the age of 13, while nearly a quarter of the 13-year-old boys who claimed to be able to remember when they had had their first real drink said that this had occurred when they were 9 years old or younger (Marsh *et al.*, 1986). However, there is a particular problem which may be encountered in trying to identify when such an event has taken place: several studies (Davies and Stacey, 1972; Aitken, 1978; Hammersley *et al.*, 1989; O'Doherty, 1988) have shown that when people are asked to recall events, their answers tend to follow a pattern. Whether the period they are asked to remember covers weeks, months or years, there is a tendency to place most events in the more *recent* past with a gradual falling away or 'recall curve' of the number of events remembered in the more *distant* past. Thus when young people are asked about the age at which they had their first drink, the older age-groups will tend to report this occurring at a later age than will younger age-groups. There is also the possibility that the respondents' definition of what constitutes a proper alcoholic drink alters with age; the glass of shandy which for the 11-year-old represented the introduction to the adult world of alcohol being forgotten by the 17-year-old to whom 'real' drinking involves downing several pints of beer. For all these reasons, it would seem to be unwise to take at face value the information that people provide about their first drink, but at the same time it is probably safe to infer that the majority of young people have at least some experience of alcohol in their very early teens. There is also substantial evidence that this first experience of drinking occurs at home and with parents (Davies and Stacey, 1972; Hawker, 1978; Bagnall, 1988).

National variations in drinking behaviour have frequently been noted by researchers. Young people in Scotland start drinking a little later than those in England and Wales; for example, Marsh *et al.* (1986) found that among 13-year-olds, 68 per cent of boys and 54 per cent of girls in Scotland drank alcohol whereas the comparable figures for England and Wales were 80 per cent of boys and 74 per cent of girls. Differences are also evident in frequency of drinking, Scottish adolescents doing so much less often than their English and Welsh counterparts. Thus 61 per cent of 17-year-old boys in England and Wales reported drinking at least weekly compared with only 47 per cent of Scottish boys of the same age. A further national difference has been found in reports of *where* young people drink. In England and Wales, a sizable minority of 14- to 15-year-olds claimed that they usually drink in a pub, whereas the numbers of Scottish adolescents in the same age group indicating this was less than half the equivalent figure for England and Wales. The Scottish adolescents, on the other hand, reported that they were *less* likely to drink at home and *more* likely to drink 'elsewhere' than their English and Welsh counterparts.

When people of all ages are asked to give details of how much alcohol they have consumed in the previous seven days, men report drinking about three times as much as women. However, the youngest age groups do not always follow this pattern and among 16- and 17-year-olds in particular, and to a lesser extent in the 18–24 age-group, there has been a tendency for women's consumption to rise in relation to men's. Nevertheless, men still drink more than women.

Deaths double in young drinkers

All kinds of alcohol and drug-related deaths are on the increase, particularly among young people.

Deaths from liver failure due to heavy drinking have doubled among young people since 1979.

While the incidence is rising in all age groups it has doubled among men and women in the 25–44 age range. The rise may be attributable in part to more accurate death certificates. Since 1984 doctors may have become more inclined to specify alcoholism because this no longer triggers an inquest.

(*Population Trends* 76, HMSO)

If we look at the drinking habits of 12- to 15-year-olds, it appears that the amount of alcohol drunk by these young adolescents remains at a moderate level, by and large. Marsh *et al.'s* 1984 survey of this age-group asked them to fill in a diary noting their consumption of alcohol in the preceding week (Marsh *et al.*, 1986). 65 per cent of the 13- and 14-year-old boys and 80 per cent of the 15-year-old boys surveyed in England and Wales said that they had drunk alcohol in that time, and the average number of units of alcohol that the drinkers claimed to have consumed during the week increased, as expected, with age, from 8.3 units for 13-year-old boys, to 11.4 units for 14-year-old boys and 15.9 units for 15-year-old boys. The comparative figures for girls were 4.7 units for 13-year-olds, 8 units for 14-year-olds and 9.1 units for 15-year-olds.

As often happens in this type of survey, there was a discrepancy between these diary figures and the responses to a question about frequency of drinking. When answering this question, only 49 per cent of the 13-year-old boys reported drinking more than a few times a year although 65 per cent went on to note some consumption of alcohol in the previous week in the diary, underlining once more the need to treat such self-reports with a great deal of caution. Nevertheless, almost half of 15-year-old girls surveyed in England and Wales reported having been 'very drunk' at least once in the previous year and half of the 13-year-old girls claimed to have been 'a little drunk' at least once during the same period.

More information is available about the drinking behaviour of older teenagers. 1989 OPCS data showed that the average number of units of alcohol that 16- to 17-year-old men reported consuming in the previous seven days was 8.1, while the combined 1987/89 OPCS figure for alcohol consumption by 'drinking' males in this age group in an average week, rather than the previous seven days, was 11.5 units (Goddard, 1991). The 1990 General Household Survey found that only 4 per cent of 16- to 17-year-old men and 3 per cent of women fell into the category of very heavy drinkers (over 50 units a week for men and over 36 units a week for women), although 13 per cent of men and 10 per cent of women reported drinking more each week than the amount categorized as 'sensible' (Smyth and Browne, 1992).

Looking at the amount of time spent drinking by people claiming to be recent drinkers – and 63 per cent of young men and 64 per cent of young women aged 16–17 reported consuming alcohol in the previous week – the combined figures for the 1987/89 OPCS surveys indicated that men averaged 4.2 hours a week. It is interesting to note that the total time spent drinking by women in this age group was the same as their male counterparts, 4.2 hours a week, but the consumption rate varied, men averaging 3.5 units per hour and women only 2.1. These differences in the drinking rates of men and women are fairly typical, and tend to be found in every age group.

If we turn to the 18–24 age group, the amounts of alcohol consumed show a marked increase and in fact this is the age at which drinking is at its highest level. The 1989 OPCS survey obtained a mean figure of 18.8 units for the amount drunk by 18- to 24-year-old men in the previous seven days, while the combined figures produced by the

1987 and 1989 surveys gave the *average* week's consumption by male drinkers in this age group as 23.9 units. 84 per cent of men of this age claimed to have had a drink in the previous week and those who drank spent 8 hours each week drinking, on average, while 73 per cent of women reported having had alcohol in the past week, the drinkers spending an average of 5.5 hours drinking. Once again the rate at which they drank differed, men consuming 3 units of alcohol an hour and women 1.9 units. The 1990 General Household Survey noted that 36 per cent of 18- to 24-year-old men reported drinking more than the 'sensible' level of 21 units a week, the equivalent figure for women being 18 per cent (Smyth and Browne, 1992), while the 1992 General Household Survey figures for this category were 38 per cent of men and, again, 18 per cent of women (Thomas *et al.*, 1994). When it came to the 'very heavy' levels of consumption, 13 per cent of men and 4 per cent of women between the ages of 18 and 24 fell into this group in 1990, the corresponding figures for 1992 showing little change at 11 per cent and 4 per cent respectively.

After the age of 25, there is a general tendency for alcohol consumption to diminish with age, fluctuating in accordance with changes in lifestyle but declining overall, until it is at its lowest point in the oldest age-group. The 1992 General Household Survey figures illustrate this tendency, indicating that 32 per cent of men and 17 per cent of women aged between 16 and 24 drank more than the recommended sensible limits whereas only 15 per cent of men and 5 per cent of women over 65 came into this category.

ALCOHOL AND OTHER DRUGS

While the focus of this book is primarily concerned with the relationship between alcohol and aggression among young people, the role that alcohol is believed to play in the onset of other drug use should be examined. Current thinking in the social psychology of drug use sees alcohol and tobacco as potential 'entry' drugs leading on to experimentation with other, illegal, drugs. Entry drugs, or drugs of 'initiation' as they are sometimes called, are therefore the first drugs that young people experiment with, before going on to use other substances. It should be noted that there is an important difference between defining alcohol and tobacco as drugs of entry or initiation and what is often called the slippery-slope theory of drug use. The slippery-slope theory of drug use asserts that experimentation with certain drugs, such as alcohol or cannabis, *inevitably* predisposes the individual to move on to use other, harder, drugs. People who use illegal and, especially, 'hard' drugs commonly report having first used 'soft' drugs, or that they started drinking alcohol and/or smoking cigarettes at an earlier age than others. Such self-reports are not counter-intuitive, but this is not the same as saying that once someone has embarked on under-age drinking, or soft-drug use such as cannabis smoking, they will therefore necessarily go on to use harder drugs.

So on the one hand, there is a growing body of evidence that early use of alcohol is associated with later use of illegal drugs (Hays *et al.*, 1987). On the other hand, however, while it is important to recognize that some young people who drink or smoke or use cannabis will go on to use other 'harder' drugs, it is also important to recognize that *most* young people who drink, smoke or use cannabis *do not* go on to use other 'harder' drugs. As a proportion of the total population the number of people that develop drug-use problems is very small.

Many people hold the popular view that the legal distinctions between alcohol and illegal drugs, such as cannabis, reflect their relative levels of harm. While the safest advice where any drugs are concerned, legal or illegal, is that any level of drug use carries some risk to health, it is not correct to say that all illegal drugs are more dangerous than all legal drugs. The harm associated with alcohol and tobacco has been well documented. On the other hand the harm associated with the use of cannabis is still a matter for considerable speculation. It seems very likely that a young person runs a greater risk of harm from heavy drinking than from moderate use of cannabis, leaving aside the obvious risk of a criminal record, a fine, or imprisonment associated with illegal drugs. To the extent that it is possible to rank the relative risks from different drug habits, it is probably fair to say that heavy drinking lies between cannabis and hard-drug use in terms of potential health risks (Donovan and Jessor, 1983).

The relationship between alcohol use and use of illegal drugs appears to be evolving in the sense that there is evidence that young people take an increasingly eclectic attitude to alcohol and illegal drugs. Thus adolescents and young adults report use of alcohol and illegal drugs in various combinations and patterns of use. Parker (1993) reported how within a representative cohort of adolescents the same young people would describe their use of alcohol for some occasions and use of illegal drugs on others. Choice of drug does not appear to be haphazard, but related to the type of event or context within which they are spending their leisure time. While drinking is still a more widespread activity than illicit drug use, the trend suggested by this research further blurs previous distinctions between what at one time would have been discrete groups of young drinkers and users of illegal drugs.

DRINKING AND DELINQUENCY

Aggressiveness and drinking are archetypal delinquent behaviours. In common usage delinquency is a broad term which ranges from offending and minor crimes to behaviours which are considered to be morally reprehensible. Understanding of youthful alcohol misuse and aggressiveness should take into account the wider range of behaviours known as delinquent or deviant behaviours with which drinking and aggression are frequently associated. Also included in definitions of delinquency are behaviours that are considered to be adult behaviours. For example, it is not considered inappropriate for adults to smoke, drink and engage in sexual behaviour. However, when adolescents and especially young adolescents do so they are considered to be inappropriately precocious. While, therefore, it is arguable that some so-called delinquent behaviours are not necessarily problematic, there are other behaviours that are inherently either anti-social or hazardous for the individual concerned. Thus experimental drinking and even intoxication are not necessarily a problem, but over--

indulgence such as drinking to the detriment of school work or to the extent of establishing a pattern of drinking that is physiologically harmful is clearly problematic. Moreover, when drinking occurs in conjunction with other problem behaviours such as aggressive behaviour then clearly this is more than simply a moral argument as to whether such delinquency is unacceptable.

Our understanding of the causes of delinquency is largely based on theories which have psychological or sociological orientations. Psychological theories emphasize the dynamics of self-esteem, interactions with peers and social aspirations. Sociological theories emphasize environmental influences such as social conditions and cultural influences. Both of these perspectives have something to offer. The origins of delinquency are most likely to involve an interaction between psychological needs and cultural influences. One avenue of research into the correlates of delinquency has suggested that deficits in social skills are correlated with delinquency (Gaffney and McFall, 1981), which suggests that early interventions could be vital to alleviate or prevent social-skills deficits from developing. A related argument might also urge early intervention where disadvantage exists to ensure the realization of potential, irrespective of the possibility that poor social skills give rise to delinquency. Other research has argued that negative social feedback giving rise to diminished self-esteem is a precursor to the development of delinquency (Kaplan, 1980). However, self-esteem explanations have recently come in for criticism as an explanation for drug use in particular (Schroeder *et al.*, 1993), which may have implications for self-esteem explanations across a number of delinquent behaviours. While there are grounds to reject self-esteem as an explanation for certain aspects of delinquency, other research has shown that delinquents frequently report perceptions of being economically and socially disadvantaged. Perceived or actual disadvantage is not a logically sufficient condition for delinquency. Nor, probably, is it a necessary condition. The nature of the causal link between disadvantage and delinquency must be mediated by other factors, reflecting intra-familial and wider cultural influences.

Another theory of delinquency is labelling theory, which states that the reaction of society to instances of bad behaviour defines for the perpetrator the future development of their self-image. For example, a young person who gets into trouble through heavy drinking becomes defined as a 'heavy drinker' or 'delinquent' by agents of social control (i.e., police, social workers, parents or whoever). The consequences of this labelling are that this label becomes incorporated into self-image: he or she believes they are deviant and this can lead, the theory states, to increased deviant behaviour. In non-jargon terms, this means that such a person is more likely to repeat or increase the deviant behaviour if they are labelled by society as deviant, because they are fulfilling their own and society's expectations of how a heavy drinker behaves. Thus the role that is fulfilled is the role as defined by reactions to the original behaviour.

This theory is in many ways over-simplistic, because it is not always clear that the dynamic nature of the development of self-image has been taken into account. Doubtless the way in which society reacts to delinquent behaviour will have some influence on the perpetrator. But the power of this influence will vary between individuals and there is some evidence to suggest that there are also important sex differences (Ray and Downs, 1986, for example) such that females may be more reluctant to adopt a deviant label than males. Moreover, the researchers found evidence to suggest that females did re-label themselves as deviant, but as a consequence of their own perceptions of their behaviour, not as a consequence of being labelled by society.

The influence of society's reaction to deviant behaviour is best seen as part of a complex framework incorporating self-image, the way in which different agents of social control react to deviant behaviour (parents might react differently from the police, or from social workers etc.), the reaction of peers, and how the individual perceives the consequences of their behaviour.

In many ways it is wrong to talk about drinking and delinquency in terms of alcohol causing delinquency. It is also possible, and perhaps more plausible, to see misuse of alcohol or other drugs as a facet of delinquency. After all, misuse of alcohol or other drugs is *in itself* problem behaviour, just like anti-social behaviour such as hooliganism. Both forms of delinquency reject social norms that emphasize 'good behaviour'. Recent research (Lavelle *et al.*, 1993) examined the relationship between personality traits, substance misuse and delinquency. This research supports the view that personality traits linked to substance misuse and to delinquent behaviour develop together, and that substance misuse is an aspect of delinquency.

PERSONALITY AND SELF-ESTEEM

The notion that young alcohol misusers are somehow different from the rest of us has been investigated by psychologists for several decades. Much of this research has been incorporated into the development of alcohol and drug education. In particular an apparent association between young people's personality characteristics such as their feelings of self-worth (self-esteem or sense of well-being) and their pattern of drinking has suggested to many investigators that those who misuse alcohol are more likely to be low in self-esteem. Research carried out in the early 1970s emphasized that young problem drinkers placed less value on achievement and had lower expectations of achievement, as well as having greater tolerance for personal deviance (Jessor *et al.*, 1972), and similar findings were obtained in a separate and more recent study (Mayer, 1988).

While there are some differences between these examples of research carried out on the personality characteristics of young alcohol misusers, the common threads are sufficiently clear in showing that young problem drinkers seem to value themselves less than other young people. Furthermore, this link has been the basis for a lot of interest in the idea that low self-worth is somehow the *cause* of problem drinking in young people, with the implication being that if you can rectify the self-worth deficit then you will prevent the development of problem drinking. This is also the basis of recent developments in drug education methods (Coggans *et al.*, 1991b;

Davies and Coggans, 1991a; Botvin *et al.*, 1990; Jessor and Jessor, 1977).

Reference has already been made to the work of Schroeder *et al.* (1993), who reviewed the literature on the causal role of self-esteem deficits in substance misuse. While the interested reader will follow up the citation, a number of their key points are worthy of repetition here, given the centrality of self-esteem explanations in this area. Having reviewed over seventy academic papers and research reports linking low self-esteem with substance misuse, they found that much of the research was methodologically and statistically flawed. For example, it was shown that across a large number of the studies reviewed the amount of variance in substance use explained by self-esteem was 'only a very small amount'. Coupled with other studies that found no link between self-esteem and substance use, the authors concluded that results were at best mixed and strongly indicated no association.

Taking another personality tack, Lavelle *et al.* (1993) reported recently that despite the shortcomings of personality theories as an explanation for drug addiction or dependence, feelings of worthlessness/unhappiness and 'antisocial' tendencies were associated with drug dependence, and to some extent with use of illegal drugs among young people. However, their own investigations strongly suggested that young people with such a personality profile were no more likely to increase or maintain their drug use than young people who were not unhappy or antisocial. Despite the focus of this research being on illegal drugs it is possible to generalize the principle of the relationship between personality traits and actual behaviour to the domain of alcohol. In other words, caution should be exercised by parents who learn that their children have been 'diagnosed' as having anti-social tendencies or low self-esteem. Such children will not inevitably develop alcohol or drug problems, though it would be wise to take such reports as evidence that at the very least attention should be paid to ensuring that any unnecessary negative influences on the child are removed and that all possible ways are explored to reinforce positive feelings. This is important irrespective of whether the young person has demonstrated any interest in misusing alcohol or other drugs.

It is perhaps surprising that personality characteristics such as hostility or aggression have not been as well researched over recent decades as other factors located in the social domain rather than the individual. This probably has more to do with trends or fashions in research than it has to do with personality factors being a fruitless research avenue, although there are many psychologists who regard 'personality' profiles as simply being a history of *how* people have behaved, rather than a description of the underlying *causes* of their behaviour. Some early studies reported that problem drinkers were characterized by being hostile, depressed and impulsive (MacKay, 1961); that pre-alcoholic adolescents were outwardly self-confident, aggressive, active rather than passive, and independent (McCord and McCord, 1960); or unstable, unpredictable, impulsive and extroverted (Jones, 1968 and 1971). These characteristics have also been found in other studies (Williams, 1970; Mayer, 1988).

While the argument as to whether personality characteristics such as the foregoing are causes of behaviour or covariants of behaviour has still to be conclusively resolved, the balance of evidence suggests that to a large extent certain personality traits develop along with the development of behaviour. Nonetheless, knowledge of the development of personality traits could be useful as a way of identifying those likely to become problem drinkers or drug users, before they come to the notice of authorities as a consequence of behaviour likely to result in prosecution.

CHAPTER SUMMARY

In this chapter we have touched on some of the major issues surrounding the problem of alcohol and disorder among young people, including the incidence of alcohol use among young people, delinquency in general and the wider context of misuse of alcohol and other drugs. In the chapters that follow we shall discuss some of the key issues that arose in more depth. In the next chapter we shall look at the nature of aggression itself. Subsequent chapters will explore the extent to which alcohol can be shown to be a cause of aggression. The final chapters will look in some detail at the role of peer pressure, and at responses to aggression.

3
AGGRESSION

INTRODUCTION

In the previous chapter we looked at a number of the main issues in relation to alcohol and violence among young people. In this chapter we shall look more closely at the nature of aggression and violence itself. At the outset it should be recognized that the problem of aggression and violence amongst young people is not somehow different from the problem of aggression and violence in society in general. Certainly age is a factor inasmuch as violent behaviour is not evenly spread across the age range, and young males in particular account for a disproportionate number of violent acts, both as perpetrators and as victims. Moreover, there are differences between males and females such that males are more likely to be involved in the commission of violent acts and to be on the receiving end. These age and sex differences notwithstanding, young people's violent and aggressive behaviour is best understood as an integral part of violence and aggression in society as a whole, even if the causes of violence in general are unclear (Walmsley, 1986; Pearson, 1988). Thus many of the features of aggression and violence exhibited by young people are no different from those exhibited by older people. The physiological, emotional and behavioural features of aggression are the same. It is just that young males account for more instances of aggressive and violent conduct, for reasons of maturation, learning and youth culture. People do not grow up in a social vacuum; each individual is the result of a complex interaction between their personality, their particular history, the culture in which they grow up, their peer group(s), role models and so on. This chapter will explore the nature of aggression and violence, with particular emphasis on why people are different in the extent to which they behave aggressively, whether under provocation or not. To understand the nature of aggression and violence involves answering a number of questions. What do we mean by aggression? Are there different types of aggression? Where does aggression come from?

WHAT DO WE MEAN BY AGGRESSION?

Every day there are stories in newspapers and on television about violence and aggression, often of a nasty and brutish nature, perpetrated on victims some of whom are wholly innocent as well as some who are perhaps more culpable. To understand the impact that aggression can have on victims it is important to define what we mean by 'aggression'. Clearly, aggressive acts are not only those that involve extreme violence with a weapon. Moreover, people can be affected differently by the same sort of incident. One person might recover quickly with no lasting psychological damage from a relatively serious assault, while someone else might be severely traumatized by an incident involving little actual bodily harm. Aggression takes many forms and can be thought of, though perhaps over-simplistically, as a continuum ranging from relatively mild verbal aggression to life-threatening physical violence. The question is not simply whether there are differences of kind or differences of degree in an objective sense. Rather it is also a question of recognizing that there are subjective differences in the perception of harm.

It is helpful to have a working definition of aggression which takes account of the range of behaviours, both verbal and physical, which can have an impact on a victim. In addition, this definition should distinguish between behaviour that is intended to harm and behaviour that *accidentally* harms someone. To encompass the range of aggressive behaviours perpetrated on victims the following definition of aggression is offered: *An aggressive act is any act of behaviour, physical or verbal, that is intended to injure someone psychologically or physically.*

The old saying about sticks and stones being more injurious than words is rather wide of the truth, for there are many cases of people suffering through threats alone, even if no physical blow is ever struck. It is therefore possible to broaden out the above definition to include the notion of aggression being any behavioural act, physical or verbal, which is *perceived* by the victim to be aggressive. This broader definition would be appropriate in certain circumstances: for example, if the purpose of the definition is to assist in determining the prevalence of any sort of aggression-related stress amongst a workforce, then it makes sense to use a definition that does not impose a framework that might not be sufficiently sensitive to the nature of the circumstances under investigation. For the purposes of this book both definitions will be used. The first, based on the perpetrator's *intention* of harm, will be useful when the emphasis is on explanation of perpetrators' motives, emotional state or personal history. The latter definition, based on the perception of the victim, will be useful when we are trying to understand how best to avoid making matters worse in the face of aggression or apparent aggression from another.

This distinction between perception of aggression and intention to commit aggression is not intended to suggest that aggression is all in the mind of the victim. First, and with particular reference to the psychological impact of aggression, perceived aggression can be extremely debilitating in a very real sense, irrespective of the intentions of the perpetrator. Second, and this is often true of groups of young people who engage in more ritualistic aggression, what appears to be aggressive behaviour might simply be acts of bravado with little intention that violence should arise.

It is also important to clarify what we mean by aggression in relation to concepts of inappropriate or bad behaviour. It might be thought that our definition should clearly state that aggression is morally reprehensible behaviour, as it is a transgression of social norms of good behaviour. The problem here is that aggression is not always inappropriate or wrong, despite the implication in our definition above that aggression is wrong when it involves the intention to cause harm or the perception of harm by a victim. When we consider issues of self-defence it soon becomes obvious that there are circumstances in which aggressive or violent actions would be considered to be morally justified. And, of course, people differ in what they consider to be morally justifying circumstances. For example, while some people firmly believe that standing up for yourself is justified, others believe in 'turning the other cheek'. Opinion will also differ about the degree of force to employ in self-defence. The upshot of this is that the morality of aggression is a substantive topic in its own right and for the purposes of this book is an aspect of aggression that will be touched on only where appropriate. Which is not to say that the moral dimension to aggression is in any way unimportant. Rather it is a recognition that in this book we need to focus primarily on understanding the nature of aggression, the role of alcohol, explaining the problems that arise, and looking at ways of responding to aggression.

Aggression, then, is usually defined as behaviour intended to harm someone, though sometimes it can usefully be defined in terms that take account of the victim's perception of harm. While it is possible for people to perceive aggression where none is intended, it is also possible that behaviour intended to appear aggressive is also not intended to turn into actual aggression, as with ritualistic displays of aggression. There can also be a moral dimension to aggression: whether aggression is justified or not. In some cases it will be, but in many other cases moral justification will not stand up to much objective scrutiny.

DIFFERENT TYPES OF AGGRESSION

For someone on the receiving end of a violent attack it might seem a bit academic whether they were attacked during a robbery or whether the perpetrator was emotionally disturbed. The result may still be physical injury and/or psychological trauma. Nonetheless, there are different sorts of aggression and it can make a difference to a victim if aggression is used as a way of carrying out a robbery or if it arises out of someone's hatred for their victim. These different categories of aggression are known as *instrumental* and *emotional* aggression.

Instrumental and emotional aggression

Aggression is often employed as a means to an end. This is most easily understood in cases of robbery where the motivation is to acquire money or valuables and victims are beaten up or injured with a weapon in order to persuade them not to offer any resistance. Perhaps the distinction is more subtle in cases, for example, where victims are beaten up by a group of youths who are motivated by a desire to demonstrate that they are 'hard', rather than doing so simply because they gain pleasure out of the act of harming the victim. The instrumental nature of some aggressive acts derives from the purpose underlying their commission. Thus, if the objective is not simply to cause harm, but is to achieve some other goal such as status, economic advantage or dominance, we would define this as *instrumental* aggression.

Aggression and violence take many forms

'It was an ordinary, quiet night in the bar. This guy just walked in and went up to him, pulled a knife and cut his throat. He [the perpetrator] didn't even know who the poor bastard was.'

(Barman's report of knife attack)

'He'll use violence if he has to. But the thing is, it's like business. He even makes a point of telling them it's not personal.'

(Police Constable's report on known 'enforcer')

Sometimes it is not easy to identify the motives of violent people. The group of youths mentioned above may include some who attack as a means to the end of achieving a sense of dominance or demonstrating toughness. It is also possible that the group might include youths who attack because they enjoy the act of harming victims. That is, aggression and violence can be an end in itself, as well as sometimes being a means to an end. Various terms have been used to describe the sort of aggression that is an end in itself, including hostile aggression (e.g. Feshbach, 1964), affective aggression or emotional aggression (Berkowitz, 1993). 'Emotional aggression' is a useful term, to distinguish the type of aggression that arises out of a state of arousal, the sole purpose of which is to harm someone or something, from instrumental aggression, the purpose of which is to achieve some ulterior goal.

Instrumental aggression can also be thought of as being more rational than emotional aggression in the sense that there is some sort of conscious awareness of a goal other than the infliction of pain itself. Emotional aggression is not so much driven by conscious thought as satisfying a need to inflict pain. At this point it is perhaps worth considering the ways in which we sometimes explain violent acts. For instance, we have all heard explanations such as 'it's just the way they are' or 'it was a motiveless attack', which suggests that the perpetrators concerned were simply born that way and there was no reason for the attack. In fact such explanations are usually wide of the mark. While there are cases of violent behaviour, committed both by sober people and by drunk people, in which there appears to be some sort of physiological defect over which the individual has no control, such cases are very rare.

Usually what is meant by a motiveless attack is that there was no apparent reason, such as stealing money or other valuables. Such cases are more properly described in terms of the motivation being *unknown* rather than being motive*less*. Without condoning such behaviour, there is in all likelihood a history of personal experiences that can explain, if not excuse, aggression and violence.

Frustration, anger and aggression

Much has been written about the role of *frustration* in aggressive behaviour and in many ways it can be seen as a classic precursor to violent incidents. Early work on the precursors to aggression in the late 1930s and early 1940s (Dollard *et al.*, 1939; Miller, 1941) put forward the frustration–aggression hypothesis to explain the role of frustration in aggressive behaviour. In this formulation frustration was defined as being the obstruction of behaviour directed towards the achievement of a goal, resulting in a state or drive that predisposed the individual to commit an act of aggression. At the time this state or aggressive drive was conceived of as being not unlike other drives such as hunger or sex in which the state of being hungry, say, resulted in a drive to seek out nourishment. However, this has been widely criticized for two reasons. First, frustration does not give rise to all instances of aggression. People often become aggressive for other reasons, as in instrumental aggression. Second, while aggression is often the result of frustration, people can also respond to being obstructed in their goal-directed behaviour in different ways, including non-aggressive ways. A great many studies have looked at the role of frustration as a *cause* of aggression, with varying results. For example, early work by Buss strongly supported the view that frustration does not always lead to aggression. The same researcher has also demonstrated that frustration can lead to behaviour that is designed to tackle the obstruction to goal achievement (Buss, 1961).

Certain aspects of the frustration–aggression hypothesis have proved to be more durable. If the frustrated person does entertain thoughts of aggression towards the origin of the obstruction other factors may have a bearing on this person's actions. For example, if he or she fears that some sort of punishment might ensue, there is the possibility that they will opt instead for a more indirect form of aggression, such as attacking property or taking it out on someone else, by way of substitution. In retrospect these elements of the original frustration–aggression hypothesis are not only more durable in terms of the complex nature of human aggression, but are also somewhat at variance with the notion that frustration gives rise to an appetite-like drive to commit acts of aggression. Only by incorporating the reality of the human as an organism that *learns* can any explanation of frustration be valid. Thus people can learn to achieve their goals by the use of force (instrumental aggression) and they can learn to gain gratification from the act of harm itself (emotional aggression). On the other hand, they might learn to gain their objectives by means other than aggression and they may never find reward in harming someone or something.

Arousal and aggression

The above qualifications about frustration notwithstanding, frustration can and does play a role in aggression. And, from the point of view of having to deal with agitated and angry people, it is essential to grasp the very real role that frustration does play in potentially violent circumstances. In some situations all that is needed is to remove the frustration from the situation, either to calm a situation down or to prevent it recurring. Experimental studies have established that preventing people from achieving a goal gives rise to an emotional state often referred to as *heightened arousal*, which can be a sufficient though not necessary precursor to aggressive actions.

The importance of the availability of options in the face of frustration was underlined in a study by Moser and Levy-Leboyer (1985) who observed the way people responded when confronted by a public telephone which did not work. In addition to the non-working telephone, two different sets of circumstances were used with unwitting members of the public; they either (a) lost their money and there was no information as to where they could find another phone and/or obtain a refund, or (b) they lost their money and information was presented in the telephone box as to where they could find another phone and how to go about claiming a refund. Members of the public were observed clandestinely. Where no information was available about alternative courses of action there were significantly more instances of aggressive behaviour, on the part of the frustrated people, towards the telephone equipment or telephone box. Typical aggressive behaviours included hitting or kicking the equipment. While it would be absurd to conclude on the basis of this study that without specific information being available vandalism will result, and the authors of this paper did not make this claim, it is clearly supportive of the general idea that lack of options can lead to aggressive behaviour.

The importance of the role of frustration lies both at the theoretical level in explaining a range of aggressive acts and at the practical level for how we should respond to aggression. Responding to aggression will be discussed in detail in Chapter 6, 'Responses to aggression'. For now the reader is asked to consider the following point. Reducing or removing frustration from difficult or aggressive encounters will lessen the likelihood that violence will occur. Moreover, reducing or removing frustration from the not-so-serious encounters which give rise to arguments will contribute significantly to lessening the likelihood that a minor dispute will escalate into a verbal slanging match, or into an even more serious problem. Where aggression is not instrumental, or part of a premeditated plan, there is often much that can be done to prevent the encounter from becoming more heated: in other words it is often possible to keep the lid on it. This requires understanding of the dynamic psychology of the interpersonal encounter or, in plain language, doing what will best result in lowering aggression. This can be a more subtle point than some would think, because to be effective sometimes requires that people reappraise their approach to aggression. More of this in Chapter 6.

WHERE DOES AGGRESSION ORIGINATE?

We have already looked at the role of frustration in the origin of aggression and recognized that frustration is a sufficient but not necessary precursor to anger and aggression. To understand why some, but not all, people react to frustration with aggression it is necessary to look at the multiplicity of influences on an individual's personal development.

In order to grasp what is meant by frustration being a sufficient but not a necessary condition for aggression we need only look at people who respond to frustration with behaviour that is intended to remove the source of frustration in a more positive or constructive way; whereas others lash out aggressively at whatever or whoever is nearby to no constructive effect. In other words, why do people differ in their normal repertoires of behavioural responses to frustration? If, for example, someone's normal repertoire of behaviour includes skills in reasoning with people, they are probably more likely to employ this sort of response, at least in the first instance. If, on the other hand, someone's usual repertoire of behaviour includes aggression, then they are more likely to respond with aggression. This level of explanation is to a large extent tautologous. If we go beyond this level of explanation to look at what gives rise to 'normal repertoires of behaviour' we can see that, in the context of frustration, this does indeed make sense.

People develop their repertoires of behaviour through a process of learning and socialization, assuming that we are talking about the great majority of people who do *not* have some sort of physiological problem that predisposes them to violence. Moreover, associated with the normal repertoire is a sense or awareness of what is appropriate behaviour under given circumstances. That is, in addition to social and linguistic skills, attitudes and beliefs play an important part in the origin of aggressive or non-aggressive behaviours. Consider the beliefs and attitudes of a young man who grew up in a culture which required that a man should respond to insult with physical threat or even attack. It is probable that such a young man has learned not only that it is appropriate to respond with violence but also that physical force can achieve the desired outcome of dominance, at least on some occasions. Thus, the hypothetical young man has been rewarded for this sort of response in the past and may never have tried other non-aggressive strategies, far less learned that these could produce a useful result.

Early experience is clearly important in the development of behavioural repertoires. We learn from observing others, particularly those that we might call role models (i.e., individuals whose behaviour is imitated because it is thought to be the most desirable or appropriate), how to respond when in similar circumstances ourselves.

Family background

There is a great deal of evidence that young people, particularly young males, in serious conflict with the law are more likely to be aggressive than those who are not in such trouble. Being highly aggressive has often been associated with other anti-social behaviours. In the light of this it is not surprising that aggression and drinking can be found together, despite the fact that alcohol in itself is not sufficient cause for aggressive behaviour. To understand why some young people develop aggressive, and other anti-social, tendencies it is important to look at the early experience of socialization, within the family for example. It is important to grasp that what is meant by the 'family' in this context is a looser definition than the nuclear grouping of mother, father and siblings all biologically related. For the purposes of this discussion the family means the immediate social grouping within which the individual develops. This might be a 'traditional' unit, a single-parent family, foster or adoptive family, being raised by a grandparent or other relative. To put it simply the important factor here is the immediate social grouping within which the child is socialized: their proximal socio-cultural influences or micro-culture.

From the perspective of early formative experiences that give rise to aggressive or anti-social people it is the quality of the relationships that matters, not their biological status (Schaffer, 1977). Before moving on to the key features of family relationships in more detail it is essential that the reader grasps the multi-factorial nature of psychological and social development. Multi-factorial development is a rather grand way of saying that many different influences interact with each other and with the individual in the development of relatively enduring behavioural traits. The list of possible influences on development is clearly extensive and would include factors such as rejection by one or more parents, being physically abused, being encouraged to be aggressive by parents, wider social norms for acceptable levels of aggression in the community, perhaps genetic inheritance and physiological characteristics. The point is that while any one of these factors might be critical in the development of an aggressive person, it is much more likely that a number of these factors will have contributed to the development of anti-social ways. It is also worth noting that, for negative factors to have a significant impact on a child's development (being physically chastised or rejected by a parent, for example), such factors have to be present on a sustained basis for lasting negative results to occur. It is the overall tone of the relationship that a young person has with his or her parents that matters, not the occasional or out of character angry reaction to misbehaviour. The odd lapse from ideal parenting will not give rise to a psychopath.

Families do have an important influence on a child's potential for anti-social development. This has been demonstrated by many studies over the years. One famous study of anti-social boys assessed family relationships in the early 1940s and re-contacted the participants many years later in the 1970s. This study revealed that in about 75 per cent of cases, of those who had a history of crime in adult life, their criminality could be explained by the ways in which their parents had treated them as children (McCord, 1979 and 1986). While some caution is appropriate with retrospective data of this sort it does suggest the possibility of parental mistreatment as an important factor in the origins of later criminality.

There is considerable debate over the physical punishment of children. Opponents of physical punishment argue that frequent physical punishment is associated with a greater likelihood of violent response from children either to their siblings or to their parents. Those in favour of physical punishment argue that it is the only way to teach children right from wrong. While it is difficult to point to specific events in someone's past that caused them to be an aggressive person, early experience of a social environment characterized by aggression and violence can be a predisposing factor in the development of aggressive tendencies (e.g. Oliver, 1993). On the other hand doubts have been expressed about the validity of retrospective claims of childhood mistreatment as the cause of abusers' own mistreatment of their children (Egeland *et al.*, 1988). Oliver's review (1993) suggests that amongst those who were physically abused as children about one-third will go on to abuse their own children, one-third will not, and the remaining third will be vulnerable to a range of social stressors and individual factors which could precipitate abusive behaviour on their children. There appears to be a very real risk factor of inter-generational transmission operating in some families which predisposes children to have inappropriate attitudes towards aggression.

The precise mechanisms by which the inter-generational transmission of abuse will operate is difficult to pin down in individual cases. Nonetheless, it is possible to paint a broad picture on the basis of well-established psychological principles. The greatest problems with physical punishment are likely to arise when, as is so often the case, physical punishment is extreme, inconsistently applied and one feature of a parenting style that also includes cold and hostile attitudes. Many if not most parents reading this section will be inclined to think that the above comments do not apply to themselves – after all it is usually *other* people who are unreasonable. Moreover, when experts in the field disagree about the use of physical punishment we tend to continue with practices that appear to work. Nonetheless, there are a number of general points concerning the impact of physical punishment to consider. First, the use of force, whether by parents or children, tends to be rewarding for the perpetrator inasmuch as it often results in what psychologists call negative reinforcement. That is, force is often employed to stop some behaviour that annoys or angers. When the annoying behaviour, or aversive stimulus, is removed by the exercise of physical punishment the person doing the punishing is rewarded by removal of the aversive stimulus.

While negative reinforcement is rewarding for the punisher the fact remains that the individual being punished has had physical pain inflicted on him or her, not to mention the psychological impact of physical punishment. Although most of those people seeking proscription of physical punishment and those who reject such abolition differ about the use of any physical punishment at all, they frequently agree about the inappropriateness of physical punishment that involves pain that is greater than a minor and very temporary discomfort. The emotional aggression and pain that may also be part of such an environment could also influence the child's development in a negative way. People who experience this sort of punishment as children will probably grow up to incorporate physical punishment as part of their repertoire of behaviour.

CHAPTER SUMMARY

In this chapter we have looked at the nature and origins of aggression, with particular regard to the role of frustration and arousal. Particular note was made of the fact that frustration does not necessarily lead to aggression and the influence of early experience was discussed. In the next chapter the relationship between alcohol and aggression will be further examined.

4

ALCOHOL AND AGGRESSION

GENERAL ISSUES

Alcohol as a cause of aggression

In the last chapter we looked at some of the features of aggression. In this chapter we turn to the links between alcohol consumption and aggression, which is an area where fact and fiction have become conflated in the public mind.

At an intuitive level most people would agree that alcohol affects people differently. For example, most of us know people who become argumentative or even aggressive when intoxicated, and we also know others who either don't behave aggressively or who become maudlin after drinking. Yet many people also believe there is a simple causal connection between alcohol consumption and aggressive behaviour. Statements to this effect are commonplace in discussions of public disorder. As we will see below, the link between alcohol and aggression is not as simple as some would think.

It is widely believed that alcohol *causes* aggression in the sense that people are more likely to become aggressive or even violent if they drink alcohol. Yet the evidence for this is less sound than many would assume. Theoretical models of causal relationships between alcohol and aggression include mediating variables, which are presumed to interact with alcohol, such that it is assumed the interaction between alcohol and one or more mediating variables determines whether or not an individual will be aggressive after consuming alcohol. Intervening variables include both individual factors such as personality characteristics, expected effects of alcohol, and situational factors including perceptions of the environment. While research has shown that the relationship between alcohol and aggression is complex, mediated by personality, alcohol-related expectancies, situational and socio-cultural factors, the precise mechanisms mediating between alcohol and aggressive behaviour remain unclear (Fagan, 1990).

Nonetheless, aggression and violence is a recurring social problem and alcohol is frequently involved. Many incidents are reported, on an apparently daily basis, including aggression on a large scale such as that associated with gangs, violence within the family or so-called 'motiveless' crimes of violence involving innocent victims. While aggression and violence take many forms, one common factor is the consumption of alcohol prior to the commission of aggressive acts (Collins, 1982; Myers, 1982; Tinklenberg, 1973).

The effects of alcohol on mood were discussed in the Royal College of Psychiatrists report *Alcohol and Alcoholism* (1979) which stated that alcohol intoxication is associated with 'impulsive violence'; that after drinking 'people get involved in more arguments' and 'assaults are also more frequent'. It has also been argued that the role of alcohol in wife-beating is 'complex' and that it would be 'erroneous to accept the argument that the behaviour of men who beat their wives is simply dictated by drink' (Dobash *et al.*, 1987).

Marsh *et al.* (1978) described how encounters between groups of football supporters are frequently ritualistic in nature; and how those who become involved in 'football violence' often drink alcohol prior to encounters with rivals. Alcohol consumption was seen as a necessary part of this football sub-culture, an essential aspect of the culture and an expression of manliness. During encounters between rival groups of fans much of the aggression and violence was ritualized with no clear willingness to become involved in actual violence. Sometimes, of course, actual violence occurs but this appeared to be more accidental than intended, given that encounters were usually conducted according to 'rules of engagement'.

While such groups report drinking prior to violent or ritualistic encounters this type of evidence cannot be taken as clear evidence for the causal role of alcohol in the origin of aggression. It is possible that alcohol has the effect of making ritualistic encounters more likely to end up in actual violence. It is also possible that alcohol is just something that people with aggressive intentions do as one aspect of their expressions of manliness in a day that is to all intents and purposes dedicated to expressing manly 'virtues'. More recently Hammersley *et al.* (1988) found that heroin and other drugs, especially alcohol, were related to crime. However, the relationship was not simply one of heroin or alcohol causing crime. Rather it seems that heroin use, and alcohol for non-users of opioids, escalated *previous* criminality. Although there is little doubt that many perpetrators of aggression are intoxicated, the precise nature of the causal relationship between alcohol and aggression is not clear.

The role of national cultural characteristics was highlighted in a recent report which drew on the views of bar workers and 'punters' in several European countries (Marsh and Kibby, 1992). There appear to be important cultural differences between different European countries, in terms of the socio-contextual factors which can influence alcohol-related aggression in public settings.

While at one level it is fairly obvious that there will be cultural differences between countries, there is no doubt that the importance of cultural differences both at a national level and at a local level has played a part in the development of drinking practices and in the development of regulations, the intention of which is to prevent excessive and inappropriate consumption. For example, relaxation of licensing laws in Scotland in 1976 was an attempt to influence drinking culture positively with the introduction of less restrictive opening hours for licensed premises. While structural aspects of public access to alcohol can be addressed through legislation, tackling the more amorphous creature of drinking culture at a local level is much more difficult. By and large good practice in preventing trouble and dealing with it when it occurs has been left to licensees, with the possibility of having their licences withdrawn being an important source of motivation for licensees to police their own premises. The overall viability of this approach notwithstanding, there are demonstrable differences between licensed premises in terms of the degree and frequency of aggression and violence experienced (MCM Research, 1990).

Previous research

The link between alcohol consumption and aggressive behaviour has been the subject of many correlational and some experimental studies. The results of correlational studies have shown that there is a relationship between alcohol and aggression to the extent that they are *associated*. These studies relied on retrospective associational procedures such as examination of police and court records to discover whether alcohol had been consumed (Wolfgang and Strohm, 1956; Voss and Hepburn, 1968; Virkhunen, 1974); or interviews with men entering prison following conviction for crimes ranging from assault with a weapon to murder (Mayfield, 1976). While these studies showed that alcohol had been consumed by high percentages of those convicted (53–79 per cent) prior to commission of violent crimes, several problems remain as a result of the study procedures.

The fact that alcohol has been drunk is only evidence for an *association* between alcohol and aggression, not evidence for aggression being directly *caused* by alcohol. Not least of the problems in drawing firm causal conclusions from these studies is that data are not presented to show the percentage of people who had consumed alcohol but who were not aggressive. Given the high proportion of people in the general population that drink in the normal course of events it would be surprising to find that a high percentage of aggressors had not themselves been drinking.

Another form of research into the link between alcohol and aggression has looked at indirect or verbal aggression. Here the evidence is more equivocal. In some studies higher blood-alcohol was associated with indirect and verbal aggression (Kalin *et al*., 1965; Boyatzis, 1974; Smith *et al*., 1975). In other studies indirect and verbal aggression were unaffected by alcohol level (Doleys *et al*., 1967; Kastl, 1969). And in some studies the effect of alcohol on levels of aggression was minimal (Mayfield and Allen, 1967; Pliner and Cappell, 1974).

Given that indirect and verbal aggression as measured in the studies above are not necessarily predictive of actual interpersonal aggression and violence it is essential to exercise caution in generalizing from such data to real-life situations. While the results of some studies support the hypothesis that alcohol potentiates verbal aggression, other research is somewhat remote from real-life aggression. For example, in one of the studies cited indirect aggression was assessed by use of the Thematic Apperception Test; a test with some problems of reliability and validity (Kalin *et al*., 1965).

Aggressive drunks or drunk aggressors?

'With some of them the night's not complete without a fight. You get the impression they really want to get drunk and fight.'

'Without drink they wouldn't cause half this much bother. They need the drink to give them the courage to fight. It's down to the drink.'

(Police Constables in Sussex)

Experimental studies

Some studies have used more direct measures of physical aggression. These studies measured the intensity of electric shock that a subject is prepared to administer to a simulated opponent within a competitive reaction time experiment (Taylor, 1967; Taylor and Gammon, 1975; Taylor *et al*., 1976). In summary, the general finding was that higher doses of alcohol were linked with higher levels of shock-setting than were lower doses of alcohol.

The evidence from shock-setting experiments tends to support the view that alcohol is causally related to aggression. However, as Taylor and Leonard (1983) point out, there is no simple correspondence between alcohol and aggression. It seems that aggression is 'a function of the interaction of the pharmacological state induced by alcohol and the contextual or environmental cues that impinge upon the intoxicated person'. One such cue is perception of threat of harm and in a study by Taylor *et al.* (1976) it was shown that the threat of harm was necessary before alcohol increased levels of aggression.

Another tack taken within the shock-setting approach was an experimental study which looked at the mediation of alcohol-related expectations on the relationship between alcohol and aggression (Lang *et al.*, 1975). The purpose of this was to control for the possibility that reactions to alcohol might be influenced by an individual's expectations or beliefs about the effects of alcohol. While all subjects were told they would be involved in an experiment concerning alcohol and behaviour, half were told they would receive alcohol and half were told they would not. Within each of these sub-groups half were given alcohol and half were not given any. It did not matter whether subjects were given alcohol or not; nor was the presence or absence of provocation important. Only those subjects who thought they had been given alcohol, irrespective of actual dose, were more aggressive as measured by the higher levels of shock set. This experiment indicates the importance of taking beliefs about the effects of alcohol into account. The nature of these beliefs is less clear, however, but seems to have something to do with expectations of how people should behave when intoxicated.

Another contextual cue with important mediating effects is social pressure. It has been suggested that social pressure can influence shock-setting in accordance with the nature of the pressure exerted. Thus intoxicated subjects encouraged to increase shock levels did so and intoxicated subjects encouraged to decrease shock levels did so, but minimally (Taylor and Gammon, 1976).

One of the documented effects of alcohol ingestion is cognitive functioning impairment, including impairment of memory (e.g. Parker *et al.*, 1974), complex problem solving (e.g. Huntly, 1973; Mills and Ewing, 1977) and performance on tasks that require simultaneous attention to multiple cues (Leigh *et al.*, 1975). In a comprehensive review of the literature Pernanen (1976) saw this narrowing of the perceptual field as likely to entail an intoxicated person interpreting in a random manner the actions of another person. Alternatively, Taylor and Leonard (1983) contend that an intoxicated person will attend to the most *salient* cues. When, Taylor and Leonard continue, an encounter is dominated by cues likely to increase aggression the intoxicated person will respond to these dominant cues and not to less dominant inhibitory cues, thus making aggression and violence more likely.

Alcohol appears to be causally related to aggression as measured in a number of studies employing direct aggression defined as shock-setting. The problem with this sort of experiment is that subjects are not in a real-life 'face to face' encounter with another person involving naturalistic interaction. It may well be that the higher levels of shock-setting linked to alcohol consumption are a function of the artificial experimental setting with participants being disinhibited with respect to shock-setting in the absence of a real adversary. It is possible that participants in such experiments do not believe that their opponent will in fact receive a shock. If so, then the validity of these experiments is in doubt to the extent that real-life encounters are qualitatively different. Faced with a real person it is likely that different results would be obtained.

Theoretical issues in the development of aggression

We have seen that there is conflicting experimental evidence as to the precise relationship between alcohol and aggression. Many theoretical perspectives have been brought to bear on alcohol and aggression, providing explanations from a wide variety of disciplines, as well as interdisciplinary explanations. At a fundamental level genetic explanations have been found to be inadequate in producing evidence of a predisposition to an intoxication–aggression relationship (Fagan, 1990). Reductionist perspectives in general lack the necessary comprehensiveness to take account of the multi-factorial nature of the relationship between alcohol and aggression. Thus a straightforward pharmacological approach might assume a direct effect of a substance, such as alcohol, on behaviour regardless both of intervening psychological processes and of socio-cultural influences. While the pharmacological properties of alcohol can be measured indirectly in terms of physiological indices, such essentially biological explanations are quite inadequate when explaining behaviour susceptible to the principles of learning, which occurs in a socio-cultural context.

Psycho-pharmacological perspectives have, to some extent, incorporated interaction between alcohol and intra-personal psychological mediators. Within such perspectives there is no assumption about aggression-causing properties inherent in alcohol, rather these perspectives explain aggressive behaviour consequent to alcohol consumption as arising out of complex interactions between substance and personality and/or emotions. Which is not to bring in genetic explanations underlying personality by another route: it is simply to make the point that any adequate theoretical framework must allow for developmental and situational influences on individual characteristics comprising 'personality'. In other words, when it comes to explaining alcohol-related aggression genetic explanations have not been particularly fruitful, personality explanations have some potential, but the interaction between developmental, individual and socio-cultural influences is likely to be the most helpful.

With the direct causal properties of alcohol open to question as a basis for explaining aggression, it is helpful to look at the wider social context in which drinking takes place. Moreover, it is important to take account of research which has had some success in explaining the development of problem behaviour among young people, particularly those theoretical approaches which take account of socio-cultural influences.

A great deal of research has gone into the origins and development of delinquent behaviour, including alcohol misuse and aggressive behaviour, paying particular attention to such interpersonal phenomena as the influence of peers. Psycho-social theories of delinquency have long included the multi-factorial nature of the development of various delinquent behaviours amongst young people, including misuse of alcohol and illegal drugs.

Much of this research derives from theoretical approaches developed and tested in the 1970s and into the 1980s. For example, problem behaviour theory (Jessor *et al.*, 1973; Jessor and Jessor, 1977; Donovan and Jessor, 1978) and the influential social learning approach (see below, p. 71). Yet, while the role of social influences is widely acknowledged, the empirical basis for specific conclusions has sometimes been over-simplified or distorted. For example, peer pressure is often cited as the cause of someone's delinquent behaviour, but the evidence for peer pressure explanations is very often ambiguous at best or actually evidence for peer preference (Coggans and McKellar, 1994). To put it another way, peer pressure explanations for delinquent behaviour do not explain why young people of similar inclinations prefer each other's company. The evidence for this conclusion is reviewed in some detail in the following chapter.

The issue of peer pressure versus peer preference notwithstanding, there is a dynamic relationship between the behaviour of individuals or groups and the wider setting within which that behaviour takes place. The thrust of this is that there are two factors to take into account when explaining aggressive and other delinquent behaviour: first, developmental factors that give rise to young people who incline towards delinquent behaviour and the company of other delinquents; second, the ways in which potential aggression is facilitated by the social context in which young people gather. The principles of learned behaviour suggest that when aggression is encouraged and rewarded by social factors such patterns of behaviour become more firmly established, making them more likely to recur even in the absence of further reward.

RESULTS OF A RECENT STUDY

Many of the studies reviewed above were correlational studies, in which two data sets (measures of aggression and measures of alcohol) are related within a methodological and statistical framework which does not permit the inference of causality. In many such cases the measures of alcohol consumption are based on self-reports. To assess the causal influence of alcohol on aggression under controlled conditions requires an experimental approach. However, experimental studies of alcohol and aggression pose a number of difficulties, ranging from the practical to the ethical. Practical issues centre on the problem of creating a naturalistic context within which subjects are not aware that aggression is being manipulated. Ethical issues centre on the extent to which it is acceptable to expose human subjects to aggressive and aversive stimuli. Moreover, the issue arises of the ecological validity of aggression research in which participants (subjects) are aware that aggression is under scrutiny. Or, more precisely, if the experimental subject is aware that the aggressiveness of their behaviour is being assessed then the issue of self-presentational bias will almost certainly confound the results.

A recent study funded by the Alcohol Education and Research Council tackled these issues in an experimental study of alcohol-related aggression (Coggans *et al.*, 1994). This study assessed the influence of blood-alcohol level and individual characteristics, such as personality and alcohol-related expectations, and the role of social context (termed 'aggression priming') on aggressiveness of subjects' responses to harassment by trained perpetrators. Throughout the experiment the real purpose of the work – namely, to examine alcohol and aggression under controlled circumstances – was withheld from participants until after completion of involvement when full debriefing took place. Participants were exposed to verbal aggression from role players with their responses monitored and rated for aggressiveness. The circumstances surrounding these encounters were ostensibly to do with a study of the influence of alcohol on co-ordination and advertising.

Measures of aggression were derived from behavioural responses, both verbal and non-verbal, in the face of aggression from perpetrators. These measures were related to a set of independent variables to assess the relative importance of blood-alcohol level, individual characteristics (personality, alcohol-related expectations, state–trait anger expression, and state–trait anxiety), and social context. For the purposes of this study social context was defined in terms of the presence or absence of social facilitation of aggression, also referred to as aggression priming.

This study differed from many other experimental studies of alcohol and aggression by involving real perpetrators, who were trained to present two different and standardized levels of aggression. Thus, in contrast to other experimental studies such as shock-setting experiments (e.g. Taylor, 1967; Taylor and Gammon, 1975; Taylor *et al.*, 1976), participants in the present study experienced real aggression in their encounters with perpetrators.

Interactions between participants and perpetrators took place 'face to face'. Data were therefore based on the behaviour of people who encountered what was, for all intents and purposes, real aggression and who at no time during their encounter with perpetrators realized the true purpose of their involvement. In other words, data were derived from people none of whom realized their experience was set up. Perpetrators and the researchers who rated participants' behaviour were all unaware of participants' target blood-alcohol level. Only the experimenter calculated and administered alcohol doses, if any.

Male and female recruits were allocated to one of the three levels of alcohol consumption (a) no alcohol (the placebo condition), (b) target blood-alcohol level (BAL) of 60mg per 100ml of blood, and (c) target BAL of 120mg per 100ml of blood. (The legal limit for driving with alcohol in the bloodstream is 80mg of alcohol per 100ml of blood.) After having their sense of taste dulled with mildly anaesthetic throat lozenges participants consumed the undisclosed amount of alcohol in the form of vodka (if any) diluted in a pint of orange juice and water. Actual amounts of vodka administered varied according to subject's height, weight, sex and experimental condition. Blood-alcohol level was monitored, by use of breath testing equipment (Lion Alcolmeter AE-D3), at regular intervals throughout the course of the experiment. Encounters between participants and perpetrators commenced when participants reached target blood-alcohol level.

Nature of the aggressive encounters

The term ' participant' refers to an experimental subject from whom data were gathered, including behavioural ratings of the degree of aggressiveness in their verbal and non-verbal responses to aggressive harassment. 'Perpetrator' refers to one of the trained role-players who harassed a participant in an aggressive and realistic manner. All perpetrators were unknown to participants and were recruited and trained for the experiment.

Two levels of aggression were involved which had to satisfy certain minimum and maximum criteria. The lower aggression level had to be more arousing and potentially anger-generating than mere irritation. At the same time the higher level of aggression had to stop short of being so anger-generating that participants might have feared for their safety to an unacceptable degree from an ethical point of view.

During an aggressive encounter, with a trained perpetrator who presented aggression and harassment, the basic scenario involved the perpetrator demanding access in an increasingly aggressive and insulting manner to a computer and room in use by the participant. The unsuspecting participant and the perpetrator were alone at this time. The experimenter, ostensibly elsewhere attending to another participant in another part of the building, was in an adjoining room observing the interaction through a one-way glass panel which afforded a clear but hidden view of encounters between participants and perpetrators.

The social priming of aggression consisted of the experimenter encouraging participants to perceive perpetrators as having no right to impose themselves by getting in the participant's way. The perpetrator was referred to in derogatory terms by the experimenter to encourage perception of the perpetrator as being a bit of a troublemaker. Depending on the experimental condition (i.e., whether aggression priming was present or absent) aggression priming took place some time before the key interaction occurred. In total 126 individual experimental trials were processed. Because of the numerous tasks involved, partly to mask the real nature of the event and partly to gather individual difference data, each participant required up to four hours to process from arrival to the end of their involvement, or when their blood-alcohol level returned to zero.

The data were analysed using a statistical technique for modelling causality called multiple regression analysis. Regression analyses included several independent variables to determine the predictive value of blood-alcohol level, age, sex, state–trait anger expression, state–trait anxiety, personality dimensions, alcohol-related expectancies, and the level of aggression to which participants were exposed.

Four dependent measures of behavioural response were looked at for any effects of the independent variables described above; (a) aggressiveness of verbal content, (b) aggressiveness of verbal style, (c) aggressiveness of body language and (d) overall aggression (a separate measure of the degree to which participants' behaviour overall was aggressive or placatory).

Main findings

There was no direct influence of alcohol on aggressive responses from people subjected to harassment. It is clear from this study that there is no direct causal link between alcohol and aggression. In fact blood-alcohol level did not explain any variance in the behaviour of participants. This finding supports theoretical models which hypothesize individual and contextual factors mediating between consumption of alcohol and commission of aggressive acts.

There was a strong influence of social priming of aggression, irrespective of blood-alcohol level. The implications of this are that the social context, within which intoxicated (and non-intoxicated) people interact with others, can ameliorate aggressive behaviour. In broad terms the key socio-contextual issue arising from this study is the extent to which people feel a sense of permission to behave aggressively or that an aggressive response is expected of them. The converse of this is that where people perceive the situation/context as one in which they are not permitted to behave aggressively, or that aggressive behaviour is not expected of them, they will be less likely to behave aggressively.

This can be translated into different contexts that prevail in various centres of social activity. Thus, for example, a key factor which differentiates licensed premises, otherwise similar in location and clientele, in terms of prevalence of aggression and violence would be the social cues governing permissible levels of aggressive interaction.

The major implication for individual and corporate licensees is to raise understanding of the ways in which staff behaviour and organizational factors influence customers' perceptions of expected behavioural standards. While clearly demonstrated standards of expected behaviour will not prevent all violent acts, particularly those involving premeditation, it should be possible to reduce the frequency of the more spontaneous outbreaks of aggression which lead to violence.

Finally, personality and individual expectations partially explained why some people behaved more aggressively. The study demonstrated that a certain amount of variance in aggressiveness of verbal content, verbal style, body language and overall aggressiveness was explained by individual characteristics: namely aspects of personality such as those defined by (a) 16PF personality dimensions factor Q1 (conservative/experimenting), factor H (threat sensitivity/boldness), and motivational distortion; (b) Eysenck Personality Questionnaire psychoticism and lie scale measures; and (c) expectations of the effects of alcohol, particularly the belief that alcohol causes arousal and aggression. Nonetheless, while individual characteristics explained a certain amount of the variance in aggressive behaviour, these were secondary to the more powerful influence of the presence or absence of aggression priming.

The various measures derived from personality and alcohol-related expectancies questionnaires were somewhat unstable, depending on which groups of participants were included in the regression model. Nonetheless, given (a) their secondary role compared with social influence, and (b) their broad similarities in terms of construct and criterion validity, this does not pose major problems for the conclusion that it is possible to identify individual characteristics that have some predictive value in the explanation of aggression.

Aggression priming

The aggression priming effect was the single most important predictor of aggressiveness. Aggression priming differs from other experimental studies of social influences on aggression in a number of ways. First, aggression priming is not the same as obedience, as in the famous Milgram experiments. Milgram showed in his obedience to authority studies that many people are prepared to follow instructions even when this entails hurting others (Milgram, 1974). In these experiments subjects were commanded to administer ever more severe 'shocks'. In the present study subjects were not given any explicit instructions as to how they should react to harassment. While it is arguable that they inferred some sort of permission to react in a more aggressive manner, this is considerably more subtle than in the Milgram experiments. Because of this the implications are also more subtle. It is easier (which is not to say it is always *easy*) to identify and remove overt instructions to commit aggression in social settings than it is to do the same with something which is more intangible or indirect, as with the implicit nature of aggression priming.

Second, in shock-setting experiments punishment is on the agenda as part of the ostensible purpose of the experiment. In the present study the aggressive encounters had nothing to do with the apparent purpose of the work. In this way the aggressive encounters were more 'real', which could be taken as also being more relevant to non-laboratory settings. This demonstrates that people do not need to be following explicit orders to infer that aggression is permissible.

Personality

Personality measures proved to be of limited value in this study, but in the course of determining this a number of issues were highlighted. First, the anger expression instrument was surprisingly of little discriminatory value. Identifying violence-prone people by the use of instruments such as the STAXI (State–Trait Anger Expression Inventory) is considered to be possible, though such measures will not necessarily predict actual violence as opposed to violent tendencies (Berkowitz, 1993). Moreover, studies which have related such measures to behaviour include research which essentially correlates two sets of self-report data (e.g. Deffenbacher *et al.*, 1986). Data sets of this sort cannot be considered to be independent of each other and it would be surprising *not* to find a positive correlation between self-reports of anger, even if one data set is STAXI-type self-reports and the other is a record of the experience of anger over a specific period of time (such as the week following completion of the STAXI).

Possible reasons for the lack of discrimination by the anger expression inventory may lie in the nature of the way it was administered in the study in question. The STAXI was developed to measure subjective experience and expression of anger (Spielberger, 1988). The experience of anger is conceptualized as having two components, namely state anger which is an emotional condition ranging from irritation to fury, and trait anger which is the disposition to interpret a variety of situations as annoying. Anger expression is defined and measured in terms of expressing anger towards people or objects, suppressing angry feelings, and control of angry feelings.

The aggression questionnaire used in this study differed from the standard STAXI as STAXI-type items were presented amongst other items which described aspects of behaviour *opposite* to those contained in the STAXI items. Thus aggression items were presented mixed in with more positive items. By this means participants were just as likely to see a connection with positive behaviours as with negative behaviours.

In addition to being presented amongst other, more positive items, the amended aggression questionnaire was itself presented as one schedule amongst several others, including personality and expectancies questionnaires. The aggression questionnaire was, therefore, effectively buried in an extensive and wide-ranging set of questionnaire schedules. By presenting STAXI items amongst other items this may have had implications for self-presentation. Or self-presentation bias may have operated in another way, though this is highly conjectural: answers on an instrument which has pejorative implications may well vary depending on how respondents perceive the testing context and whether this has any negative implications for themselves. In the present study every effort was made to create a testing context in which perception of 'agenda' was unclear. To the extent that this was successful, and there are the reports from participants' debriefings that they did not doubt the ostensible reason for participation, there is some basis to suggest that participants would see no self-presentational benefits in presenting a picture of themselves as aggressive.

If self-presentation influences such as the above were operating this would explain why only the more loosely related measures discriminated between people who were more or less aggressive; and why the personality measures were less stable across different subgroups of participants.

Implications for alcohol-related aggression

The principal conclusion that arises from this study is that much of what is termed alcohol-related violence may have less to do with alcohol *per se* than with the social context in which people drink, particularly people with aggressive tendencies. The question of interaction between alcohol and factors that intervene between alcohol and aggression is partially answered by this study. It would, however, be going beyond the data to suggest that only social factors influence aggression. Nonetheless, the role of social influences, of the sort revealed by this study, in the potentiation of aggressive behaviour also extends beyond isolated instances. The principles of learning suggest that social influences of this sort will also have an influence on the psychological and behavioural development of individuals. Social facilitation or encouragement of aggression will make people with aggressive tendencies more likely to repeat such behaviour in the future. While there are limits, of feasibility and desirability, to the control of social interaction there is still the question of ensuring that centres of social activity do not facilitate aggressive behaviour.

CHAPTER SUMMARY

The value of assessing the relationship between alcohol and aggression in experimental studies is to disentangle the various pharmacological, psychological and social factors that may give rise to aggression. Of central importance is the extent to which such studies can shed light on the very real problems suffered by people on the receiving end of alcohol-related violence. For example, a woman who is beaten regularly by a drunken husband will find the results of such work of only academic importance, if at all. For her the violence is real and always seems to coincide with her husband being intoxicated. What matters most to her is to stop him getting drunk and assaulting her. What relevance, she might say, do these observations have for someone in her position?

By manipulating the influence of alcohol and of social factors in the controlled manner employed in the experimental work described above it is possible to tease out the relative importance of each in the population studied. While it can be argued that the population studied was not representative of all shades of human reaction to alcohol they did represent a typical sample of young adults. The lesson that can be drawn is that, for the bulk of alcohol-related incidents of aggression, alcohol *per se* is of considerably less importance than the social influence that humans have on each other.

The type of intervention that is required for the sort of alcohol-related violence suffered by the abused wife or partner will be reactive in the sense that the violent perpetrator has already developed a pattern of behaviour that habitually involves aggression and alcohol abuse. While he may be violent every time he gets drunk it should be remembered that the violence may be precipitated by alcohol but not directly caused by it. The inclination to be violent, as well as the inclination to become drunk and violent, is the result of the many formative experiences over his lifetime. It may be little consolation that the alcohol in the bottle does not directly cause him to be violent, but the accumulation of evidence strongly indicates that this sort of person does not have to be the way he is. Some such men will be lost causes insofar as they are unwilling to change their behaviour, but others can change their ways with the help of treatment or psychological therapy. Nonetheless, while prevention may be better than cure, the task of changing the social and cultural environment to prevent or ameliorate the development of aggressive behaviour is enormous.

5
PEER PRESSURE?

INTRODUCTION

In previous chapters we discussed the nature of aggression and violence, alcohol consumption among young people, and the relationship between alcohol and aggression. The purpose of this chapter is to examine in more detail some of the formative influences on young people, in particular, the role of peers and the family. Frequently people blame a young person's bad behaviour on 'the people he/she goes around with' or 'the parents'. The term 'peer pressure' is heard constantly and is used to explain everything from smoking cigarettes to so-called joy-riding. The reason for this emphasis is that peer pressure as an explanation for delinquent behaviour has become a received wisdom despite the fact that the evidence is wanting. Most of the research on peer pressure has been in the area of substance misuse, particularly with illegal drug use. Given the relationship, described in previous chapters, between the range of delinquent behaviours it is appropriate to consider the implications of the deficiencies in the research which forms the basis for asserting that peer pressure is a major causal factor. It is not appropriate to view drinking or aggression or drug use as separate issues. The co-incidence of delinquent behaviours strongly suggests that lessons drawn from one area will have implications for others. So, while much of the evidence discussed in this chapter is drawn from drug and alcohol-related studies, the issue of peer pressure as an inadequate explanation can be seen as relevant to delinquency in general.

The thrust of the argument in this chapter is that the widely accepted influence of peer pressure is misunderstood and misplaced. [1] By and large the role of the family (or of any non-biological caretaker) is more important, especially with the development of drinking habits. However, before looking at the evidence for the importance of the family we shall first look at the evidence for the role of peer pressure in the development of delinquency in young people.

There is a tendency for drinking, drug misuse, aggression and fighting not to occur in isolation from a range of other delinquent behaviours. Young people who engage in one or more delinquent behaviours are more likely to engage in others as well, a phenomenon which has been described as the problem behaviour syndrome or proneness to problem behaviour (Donovan and Jessor, 1978; Jessor and Jessor, 1977; Newcomb and McGee, 1989). The range of problem behaviours include those that can be seen as problematic irrespective of the age at which they occur, as well as behaviours considered to be problem behaviours because they occur at an age earlier than is thought to be appropriate (such as young adolescents engaging in sexual behaviour). Thus the range of behaviours that is termed 'delinquent' in much of the literature includes alcohol or drug misuse, aggression and violence, theft, vandalism, behavioural or disciplinary problems in school or at home, sexual activity and problems with the law.

While it is not inevitable that a young person engaging in one of the above problem behaviours will also engage in the others, there is a tendency for a number of them to co-occur. There is considerable evidence to show that alcohol or drug use, petty theft, vandalism, precocious sexual activity, and a general tendency towards rebelliousness are associated (Bachman *et al.*, 1984; Donovan and Jessor, 1983; Kandel, 1980). The precise nature of the underlying cause or causes of this tendency for a range of delinquent behaviours to co-occur remains unclear, though various possibilities have been suggested: for example, that the association between various delinquent behaviours is underpinned by some sort of personality trait such as rebelliousness or low social conformity or by a 'biosocial' dimension of personality (Zuckerman and Como, 1983) such as a predisposition to sensation-seeking (based on a theory suggesting a physiological sensitivity to reinforcement reflecting catecholamine and enzyme levels); or that one delinquent behaviour such as alcohol misuse leads to (or causes) other delinquent acts such as criminal behaviour.

PEER PRESSURE

Much has been made of the importance of peer 'pressure' as a major causal factor in the onset of delinquency, including alcohol misuse, illicit drug use, confrontational or aggressive behaviour, amongst other forms of delinquent behaviour, despite the fact that most data presented as evidence for this are associational. That is, the data are correlated which simply means that their occurrence is associated, not that one factor causes the other. The co-occurrence of two factors is frequently misinterpreted in terms of one being the cause and the other being the effect. There is some attraction in peer pressure explanations because such explanations divert blame away from parents (which is not to say that parents are always to blame – very often they are not). Instead blame can be laid at the door of these influential others who are responsible for leading the young person astray. It also can serve the function of distracting attention from the role that the young person plays in his or her own development. Peer pressure explanations can be misplaced in the sense that such explanations are often interpreted as the young person being passive in the face of pressure from others. That is, he or she is unable to refuse and is therefore in some way not primarily responsible for the acts he or she has committed. In this form 'peer pressure' is a type of inadequacy theory, just as 'self-derogation' theories for illicit drug use explain drug use as some sort of compensation for low self-esteem.

While there is evidence to show that peer factors are associated with delinquent behaviour this evidence has often been inappropriately interpreted or cited as support for peer pressure when it should have been more appropriately interpreted as evidence for peer assortment or peer preference. (This is especially true of much of the research into peer pressure in drug use: the delinquent behaviour that ranks high on any poll of parents' and teachers' worries and is often assumed to lead on to stealing and violence.) If the active role of the individual is ignored then the role of peers, and the nature of interactions between individuals and peers, will not be properly understood. It is still commonplace to hear of 'peer pressure' (coercion or persuasion to do something) or 'peer influence' (a vague term indicating that the impact of peers is effectively to make others do something), when more appropriate terms would be 'peer support' (toleration, approval or encouragement of an individual's delinquent attitudes or behaviour) or 'peer assortment or preference' (favouring or choosing some friends or associates over others). The way that peer pressure or peer influence is defined in many research reports makes it clear that the researchers concerned viewed peer pressure as being only one (possibly causal) factor amongst others in a dynamic and reciprocal relationship between individuals and peers. Which means that factors other than peer pressure play a part; and any adequate explanation of drinking and aggression amongst young people will have to include individual factors such as beliefs, attitudes and aspirations, as well as other developmental and social factors such as family and culture.

Why do they do it?

'It's not really their fault, it's the company they keep.'

'They only do it because the others do it.'

'It's not that easy to make a child do something it doesn't want to.'

'Children don't turn into hooligans just to please another kid.'

(Teachers' views on problem children)

There is a need to understand the role that the individual plays in his or her own development. Individual motivation and choice of peers should not be seen simply in terms of personal or social inadequacy. It is all too easy to forget that from their own perspective the behaviour of young 'delinquents' makes as much sense to them as do the behavioural decisions of more conforming young people. It is possible to recognize this without such recognition being an acceptance of delinquent behaviour; but if we are to understand why young people do things that we might consider to be destructive, either personally or socially, then it is necessary to understand that they do so for their own reasons which they consider to be valid. That is one of the reasons why delinquency is such an intractable problem and is not susceptible to simple solutions. To counteract the strength of the influences that give rise to preference for 'delinquency' it is not sufficient to talk of (essentially trite) solutions such as 'short sharp shocks' that do nothing to lay a sound foundation for alternative and more conventional preferences. Societal responses that emphasize punishment and privation for miscreants say more about people who want to do the punishing than about the efficacy of such responses. The desire for retribution is all too easy both to understand and to fall prey to, particularly if you have been on the receiving end of destructive or aggressive behaviour. Moreover, there is the argument that the victim does not get as good a deal from society these days as the perpetrator does, and who cares about the so-called rights of the violent young thug anyway? Much of this chapter is concerned with the argument that peer pressure is an all too easy and useful explanation for delinquent behaviour and can even, in some cases, let the individual off the hook for his or her own wrongdoing. However, and this cannot be said too strongly in case the fundamental point being articulated here is not grasped, it is not appropriate to draw the conclusion that the answer lies only in personal responsibility. The point is that, while peer pressure should in most instances be re-written as peer preference, the influences that give rise to preference for delinquent rather than conformist peers lie in the early experiences of young people, in their families, in their schools, and in the culture of their communities.

A second caveat is that when we talk of the importance of early influence this refers to early influence over those aspects of individual development that can be influenced. It is not being suggested that a delinquent individual came into this world as a *tabula rasa* and became delinquent because parents or caretakers made him or her that way. In many cases parental influence may have given rise to the delinquent results before us. But it is also possible that the genetic inheritance of the young person concerned may have predisposed him or her to be problematic in some way or other. However, the genetic explanation is tenable only in certain ways. First, the existence of a 'criminal' or 'delinquent' gene is not a realistic probability. Second, genetic influences that have behavioural implications are usually a matter of tendency or degree rather than an all-or-nothing presence or absence of delinquency.

As a general rule genetic explanations are of little use in explaining delinquency. After all, young delinquents tend to grow out of their delinquency, adopting more conventional lifestyles as they get older. Young delinquents who do become more conventional as they get older do so because they have in some way come to realize, for themselves, that they want these other more conventional things out of life.

There is an all too widespread lack of recognition of the reciprocal nature of peer relationships where delinquent behaviour is concerned. This is most obvious in the area of alcohol and drug education. For example, drug education in schools (which now usually covers legal and illegal drugs) is based on models of delinquency development which place an undue emphasis on peer pressure. These models tend to become oversimplified as the theoretical research becomes transformed into educational packages, failing to take into account the reciprocal nature of relationships between young people and their peers. This results in drug education, especially school-based drug education, failing to tackle the desire of many young people to use drugs on a recreational basis because they want to do so, not because they lack knowledge, social skills or have a poor self-image. Some drug education still revolves around 'just say no' messages, so-called decision-making skills, or refusal skills. In other words, resist pressure from your peers – which will be ineffective if you actually want to do it.

Reciprocal models of delinquency, allowing for a dynamic relationship between individuals and groups, have been around for some time (e.g. Endler and Magnusson, 1976; Huba and Bentler, 1982; Huba *et al.*, 1980; Zucker and Gomberg, 1986) and some educational programmes recognize the importance of the interactive nature of the relationship between individuals and groups (Wragg, 1992). However, this reciprocal perspective has yet to make a significant impact on wider public awareness.

Baumrind (1985) asserted on the basis of her research that adolescent drug use was normative behaviour and did not arise from pathological personal characteristics or from pathogenic socialization processes. Other research supports the view that the majority of drugs users cannot be described as having abnormal personalities (Newcomb and Bentler, 1988; Reuband, 1977).

While contending that the power of peer pressure is often overestimated it is also important to recognize that, as in any dynamic and reciprocal relationship, it is the interaction between individual and social factors that defines preferred lifestyle and behaviour. It is important to recognize that just as it is often wrong to assert that people take drugs because of pressure from others, it is also wrong to assume that social factors have no influence. It is the nature of this dynamic relationship that requires to be elucidated. Evidence frequently cited as evidence for peer pressure is more properly evidence that supports a dynamic and reciprocal perspective on peer assortment, also known as homophilic assortment: that is, the coming together of social groups, which evolve and change over time, to provide a more amenable social setting for the attitudes and behavioural preferences of the individual. In other words, most young people choose their friends on the basis of similar attitudes, rather than these friends pressuring individuals into behaviour they do not really want to engage in.

PEER PRESSURE OR PEER PREFERENCE?

A considerable amount of research on peer pressure and drug use derives from theoretical approaches developed and tested in the 1970s and into the 1980s. For example, problem behaviour theory which sought to explain 'problem behaviour proneness' (Jessor *et al.*, 1973; Jessor and Jessor, 1977; Donovan and Jessor, 1978). Another influential example is the social learning approach (e.g. Burgess and Akers, 1966; Akers, 1977; Akers *et al.*, 1979), which specifically included the phenomena of 'imitation' (Bandura, 1977) and 'operant conditioning' (Skinner, 1959).

In a subsequent review (Kandel, 1980) it was noted that two of the key measures in problem behaviour theory lacked empirical clarity, namely (a) personality and (b) perceived environment (which encompassed both peer models and peer approval for drug use). Given that the two measures were 'highly interrelated and probably measured the same thing', the data cannot be said to support the notion of peer pressure. In addition, amongst a number of factors which did not predict marijuana and alcohol use was 'alienation'; suggesting either that there was no variance amongst the cohort in terms of 'alienation', or that being 'alienated' was not related to drug use. The definition of 'deviancy' used was arbitrary, given that problem behaviours included sexual intercourse, activist behaviour and drinking. Engaging in such behaviours earlier than might be considered 'normal' should not be taken as evidence of maladjustment. In all other respects concerning psychological and social adjustment they may have been quite 'normal'. Kandel, in the same review, pointed out that the social learning approach developed by Akers (Burgess and Akers, 1966; Akers, 1977; Akers *et al.*, 1979) failed to show the results necessary to support peer pressure models. While differential association and drug-related attitudes were significantly related to drug use, imitation and differential reinforcement were not. A pattern of results like this is evidence more for peer preference than for peer influence. More recent research (Akers and Cochran, 1985) tested social learning theory, social bonding theory, and anomie (or strain) theory. Social bonding and anomie variables were unimportant. Of three remaining variables (marijuana-related attitude, differential association and differential reinforcement) the least important was differential reinforcement. Differential reinforcement was concerned with friends' 'rewarding or punishing' reactions to their own marijuana use and can be more parsimoniously interpreted as reflecting preference for like-minded peers rather than peer pressure. These early social-learning findings show that young people who use drugs tend to associate with others who use drugs and that they share similar attitudes or beliefs. The data do not demonstrate that peers coerce non-drug-using individuals to join them in their habits. Given (a) the lack of specificity of personality and perceived environment, (b) the lack of relationship between drug use and imitation or differential reinforcement, and (c) an association between individual and peer drug use, these studies can more plausibly be interpreted as support for peer assortment/preference than as support for peer pressure.

Adolescents sharing the same attitudes and beliefs tend to associate with each other and subsequent drug use by a group member could be more easily explained by these attitudes and beliefs than by the influence of the rest of the group. Such an interpretation was supported by the work of Jessor *et al.* (1973) who found that adolescents who shared characteristics such as valuing independence more and achievement less would tend to form a group. They also found strong evidence for the dynamic nature of the relationship between individuals and peers. In both cross-sectional and longitudinal comparisons the researchers found that, while social support was a stronger predictor of marijuana use, 'personality is, indeed, central to variation in drug use, whether there is high social support for it or not'. The same authors noted that the role of personality variables was important, given the inclination for social theories of drug use to emphasize the role of situational factors. Although aspects of personality related to drug use were 'distal', in the sense of being related to drug use indirectly (theoretically or conceptually), these findings demonstrate the need to take intra-individual factors into account. It is also worth repeating that 'social support' is not the same thing as peer pressure.

Support can be toleration, approval or encouragement. Encouragement comes closer to the popular interpretation of peer pressure than either approval or toleration, but not so close as to constitute pressure to make someone do something they do not want to do. In fact the operational definition of social or peer 'support' has more to do with approval than pressure. Which suggests this type of measure is only indicative of shared attitudes and behaviours. A further example of this is the longitudinal examination of measures of coping through support-seeking carried out by Wills and Vaughan (1989) which found that adolescents who said that they would seek peer support in a crisis rather than that of parents or other adults were more likely to use substances. Since there was no investigation of the quantity or quality of any support which might be available to the subjects, the data really tell us nothing about actual peer support which might influence the subjects but instead appear to be measuring something akin to a personality or motivational factor; and when many researchers refer to 'peer-support' as an influence it is more accurate to refer to a *peer support-seeking tendency*.

SIMILARITY AND ATTRACTION IN GROUPS

The tendency of groups of friends to be similar in attitudes and behaviour has long been acknowledged (Newcomb, 1961 and 1962; Kandel, 1978) and the part played by the selection of similar friends in producing this group homogeneity has been examined. Cohen (1977) found that homophilic selection, the selection of friends with prior similarities, accounted for most of the homogeneity in the groups he observed, and he concluded that 'peer influence has been consistently overestimated ... since in each study some combination of effects of uniformity pressures and homophilic choice has been taken to be the effects of peer influence alone'. Britt and Campbell (1977) examined adolescents' drinking practices in relation to that of their peers and noted that 'uniformity, in short, appears to be due less to emergent group norms which generate behavioural and normative similarity than the selection of groups by individuals on the basis of imputed similarity'. Kandel (1978) estimated that the processes of selection and socialization are equally important influences on group homogeneity, and commented that models which attribute all the similarity between friends to peer influence 'overestimate by about 100% the influence of friends by failing to take into account the role of prior similarity in friendship formation'.

When the 1978 Kandel paper is re-read, some fifteen years after it was published, the naïveté of much of the intervening research is underlined. Moreover, given that both the social psychology and the sociology of deviancy (in general) have moved on considerably from simplistic deterministic models, it is perhaps surprising that this development is not reflected to the same extent in drug research. A quote from Kandel (1978) seems appropriate: 'Adolescents co-ordinate their choice of friends and their behaviours so as to maximize congruency. ... if ... the friend's attitude or behaviour is incongruent ... the adolescent will either break off the friendship and seek another friend or will keep the friend and modify his own behaviour.'

Such insights accord with investigations of social selection and socialization across a wide range of behaviours. Perhaps this is the key to the difference between explanations for drug use and explanations for most other behaviours. It seems necessary for those providing these explanations to do so in ways that fit their world-view: drug use is incomprehensible to them except in so far as it can be explained as the result of evil influence or in terms of overwhelming pharmacology. There is an extensive literature in social psychology which demonstrates the robustness of attributional functionality across many domains of behaviour (e.g. Hewstone, 1983). Attributional analyses of explanations for drug use have demonstrated that such explanations for drug use serve the psychological needs of those who made them (Coggans and Davies, 1988; Davies, 1992).

SPECULATIVE INTERPRETATIONS

Attempts to identify factors which influence the use of legal and illegal drugs by adolescents have frequently been based on associational data gathered within cross-sectional research, and used as the basis for speculative causal inferences in favour of 'peer pressure' interpretations, despite the evidence pointing in other directions. For example, in a study of influences on drinking and achievement, data collected by Biddle *et al.* (1980) found little direct effect of parental and peer pressures on adolescent drinking. However (though recognizing that various interpretations were possible), this did not discourage speculation on the mechanisms by which parents and peers may influence adolescents. White *et al.* (1986) noted that 'friends' use of alcohol, marijuana and drugs are consistently and strongly related to subjects' use', and concluded that 'these findings suggest that adolescent alcohol and drug use conforms to the behavioural and value structure of the peer influence group'. While the authors point out that they cannot claim 'these processes are causal factors', they also point out that friends' drug use and tolerance are the most powerful predictors of drug use, as well as speculating that their data might have suppressed 'strain effects' (i.e., psychological distress). Another investigation, of family and religious influences on adolescent substance abuse, found that substance use was strongly associated with the level of peer drug use (Bahr *et al.*, 1993). From this finding they reached the conclusion that 'having peers who use drugs appears to be the dominant influence on whether adolescents abuse drugs'. Other research reporting associations between individuals and peers quite incorrectly describes direct and indirect associations as direct and indirect 'causal effects' (Ried, 1989).

The desire to interpret peer associations as peer pressure, rather than peer preference, is also evident in work that developed a psychometric scale defined as a 'susceptibility to peer pressure scale', even though it was based on tolerance of deviance measures (Dielman *et al.*, 1987 and 1989). While the authors refer to the origins of the susceptibility to peer pressure scale, and to possible confusion of the two distinct concepts, they clearly prefer their interpretation of susceptibility over tolerance. Susceptibility to peer pressure is not the same as tolerance of deviance, as the former implies that the person is likely to do what peers want, while tolerance of deviance is consonant with peer preference. Moreover, the scale items do not address the issue of being pressured to do something that the respondent does not want to do, nor do they address illicit drug use.

The point at issue here is not that such examples of peer pressure/influence research deliberately mislead, rather it is that they couch their interpretations in terms that leave the reader in little doubt that the authors incline towards peer-influence interpretations. Yet the data from which they work are as much evidence for peer preference as for peer pressure. Objectivity, parsimony of explanation, and the data all require that peer-pressure inferences are eschewed. Of course, researchers are in the business of hypothesizing, but there seems to be an all too widespread unwillingness to accept that people could be motivated to use drugs for reasons other than pathological.

This tendency to prefer inadequacy theories for drug use is evident in other investigations of the social and intra-personal dimensions of drug use. Self-esteem explanations suffer from similar interpretation bias (Schroeder *et al.*, 1993). There is a widespread belief that drug use is *caused* by low self-esteem, based on correlational data linking low self-esteem with drug use. Yet, for example, when a recent lifestyle survey found an association between high self-esteem and smoking amongst boys this was explained in terms of smoking 'boosting self-confidence' (Currie and Todd, 1990), not smoking being caused by high self-esteem. So it would seem that if drug use is associated with low self-esteem this means that low self-esteem is the cause of drug use. But when drug use is associated with high self-esteem this still means that drug use is caused by low self-esteem, or to boost self-confidence. The logical flaw is obvious.

In some respects the terms 'peer influence' appears to move away from the coercive implications of 'peer pressure', but the term runs the risk of being so vague as to be unhelpful, because the nature of this influence is neither qualified nor quantified. If the purpose of such research is to shed light on the nature of the relationship between drug users and their peer networks little or nothing is added to our knowledge.

Other researchers have made progress towards more reciprocal approaches. For example, peer-cluster theory (Oetting and Beauvais, 1986 and 1987) describes peer clustering as the coming together of young people who share similar beliefs, values and behaviours. These groupings are 'smaller subsets – tight cohesive groupings – in which clearly defined attitudes and shared behaviours mark membership'. While there is a strong implication that such clusters *dictate* shared beliefs, values and behaviours, this approach can be seen as a move towards a more dynamic perspective. Drawing on a path analysis of their data the authors report that, while they cannot be conclusive about temporal sequence, their data suggest that poor school adjustment precedes drug use and influences peer associations. Moreover, they make the interesting point that schools may well facilitate the formation of (potentially) deviant clusters by bringing together less successful pupils in classes, remedial classes or detention groups.

However, in a critique of the peer-cluster approach it was argued that this essentially reductionist approach failed to account for the dynamic, longitudinal interplay between social context and individual, a failure which reflected widespread 'immaturity of scientific thinking in the area of drug abuse' (Shaffer, 1986). While arguing for non-reductionist and dynamic understanding of drug use Shaffer noted, with particular reference to marijuana, that the role of psychological pathology (which has never been clear) is a less useful explanation as drug use becomes more normalized within social contexts.

Finally, a recent longitudinal study which concluded that peer substance use is a predictor of future drug use in non-using adolescents (Stein *et al.*, 1987) also supported a multi-causal approach to understanding different patterns of drug use. The data revealed that early peer drug use was *not* associated with later disruptive or problematic drug use. The same research investigated the role of family disruption and perceptions of adult drug use on later drug use by the cohort. Family disruption was indirectly related to later drug use and there were indications that early exposure to adult alcohol use could be linked to later problematic use of alcohol or illicit drugs. Overall, this eight-year longitudinal follow-up provided support more for the influence of early socializing factors than for the role of peer pressure. Moreover, the body of research indicating that there are identifiable dimensions of personality which can be used to predict which adolescents will use drugs (see below), together with the evidence for homophilic assortment, supports the contention that dynamic and reciprocal explanations based on peer preference would be more appropriate.

INTRA-PERSONAL FACTORS AS PREDICTORS OF SUBSTANCE MISUSE

So far in this chapter discussion has centred around the 'mind-set' of much research on drug use, to the effect that peer-pressure explanations seem to be preferred even when the data suggest otherwise. It has been shown that peer preference, or homophilic assortment, is a more appropriate interpretation of existing data and has been actively supported by other research. It is not the intention here to go much beyond the issue of peer preference being a more appropriate interpretation than peer pressure. However, in the course of reviewing the foregoing research a number of intra-personal factors were clearly relevant to an understanding of why young people take drugs.

Many investigations in this field have concluded that there are measurable dimensions of personality which are characteristic of the adolescent who uses or is likely to use drugs. In her review of patterns of use of legal and illegal drugs among adolescents, Kandel (1982) noted the evidence produced by longitudinal studies that 'many of the factors found to be associated with drug use at one point in time, such as low academic performance, crime, low self-esteem, depressive mood, rebelliousness, and other personality characteristics *precede* the use of drugs' (emphasis added), and that 'the use of marijuana is preceded by acceptance of a cluster of beliefs and values that are favourable to marijuana use and in opposition to many standards upheld by adults'.

Brook *et al.* (1983) carried out a cross-sectional investigation of personality, peer and family correlates of the four stages of drug use defined by Kandel (1975): non-use; use of legal drugs; use of marijuana; and use of other illicit drugs. Not surprisingly, they found that friends' drug use and peer deviance differentiated among the four categories of drug use, but also that a non-conventional personality as measured by tolerance of deviance and rebelliousness differentiated in the same way. Eisterhold *et al.* (1979) and Yancy *et al.* (1972) reported that a majority of adolescents who had tried marijuana gave curiosity as their principal reason. Austin (1988) also noted that character was more important than peer use in predicting which adolescents would use drugs, and found that drug use in early adolescence was related to concurrent and pre-school personality characteristics. The multi-dimensional nature of drug use, including choice of drug, personality and social variables, has also been reported as well as the need to differentiate the non-problem user from the problem user (Segal, 1986).

It should not be concluded from this that drug use is caused by personality deficits. The distinction between tolerance of deviancy and non-deviant attitudes is an arbitrary, if moral, one. Moreover, some personality-deficit theories have been under attack recently for methodological problems. For example, self-derogation or self-esteem theories (the basis for much of the present-day infatuation with personal-deficiency approaches which focus on a presumed lack of self-esteem) provide a less than complete explanation for why young people engage in 'deviancy', of which drug use is but one aspect. Self-derogation approaches may have a role in explaining the more pathological patterns of drug use (abuse), but have little or nothing to contribute to explanations of why people, who are non-deviant in all or most other respects, engage in recreational drug use. The review of the relationship between self-esteem and drug use cited earlier (Schroeder *et al.*, 1993) identified a number of methodological and statistical problems with the research, including deficiencies in measurement, invalid drawing of inferences from correlational studies, and misinterpretation of data. There are parallels between self-esteem and peer pressure as explanations for drug use. Both are inadequacy theories based on assumptions that people engage in drug use because they are compensating for deficiencies in self-image, or that they lack social skills (i.e., lack the skills to resist something they really do not want).

CONCLUSIONS AND CHAPTER SUMMARY

We have seen that the evidence for peer pressure is equally, if not more appropriately, interpretable as evidence for peer preference. The foregoing argument has implications for drug education, particularly drug education based on peer-pressure interpretations of drug-use onset. The arrival of life-skills drug education was felt by many to be a useful step in the right direction. So far little evidence has come to the fore to support early enthusiasm for these approaches. This lack of impact lies not so much in the irrelevance of all of the life-skills approach, but rather that something seems to get lost in the translation between the theory and practice of such drug education (Coggans *et al.*, 1991a and 1991b; Davies and Coggans, 1991a). Prevention programmes based on resistance of peer pressure have been largely ineffective (Coggans *et al.*, 1991a) or met with mixed results, though some success has been found in relation to cigarette smoking (Elder *et al.*, 1987). Other studies indicate that more broadly based life-skills approaches may have some potential, though the impact has been found to be temporary (ACMD, 1993). Blanket approaches to drug education based on notions of inadequacy will be doomed to failure, because for the majority of those who experience drug education and go on to experiment with drugs their motivation will have nothing to do with inability to resist peer pressure or with psychological pathologies. Similar concerns have been voiced with respect to alcohol education (May, 1993).

The key issue in this chapter is that peer pressure is inappropriate and unsupported as an explanation for drug use. At the same time it has been argued that the nature of the relationship between individuals and peers is dynamic and reciprocal. A great deal of evidence has been reviewed that demonstrates the need to take individual and social factors into account. How do we take account of the social aspects of development and the dynamics of relationships between young people and those around them? Two points might help to address this issue.

First, while drug education based on simplistic interpretations of peer pressure and self-esteem is ineffective, peer preference and self-image are still considered to be key factors in the successful development of young people across the whole range of their accomplishments, whether positive lifestyle behaviours or academic achievements. In years to come it will probably be realized that to deal with social relationships and self-image in the context of 'drug' education was in some ways naïve. Educationists have long understood that such matters should be part and parcel of the entire educational, as well as the wider developmental, experience of young people. After all, why is it assumed that drug education requires sessions on resisting peer pressure and developing self-esteem, but in order to do well in other areas of skill-development it is the educational and home environments that matter? Where are the peer pressure and self-esteem sessions in English or arithmetic? There is one more aspect to this issue that must be grasped: having excellent social skills and being able to assert oneself will not preclude drug use, just as adequate or high self-esteem does not.

Which brings us to the second point. Given that peer pressure is far too limited a basis from which to approach drug education, there is clearly a need to place personal development within the wider context of educational settings. As far as school-based health education is concerned, recent developments in health education and health promotion focusing on the ways in which educational institutions co-ordinate and support holistic approaches to personal development offer more fruitful approaches. While the concept of the health-promoting school has still to take root in a widespread basis, there are encouraging developments in some areas. (This lack of widespread development stems largely from competing curricular and pastoral demands on schools, as well as a certain lack of profile and importance at both national and local levels, not from intrinsic shortcomings in the concept itself.) While specific messages concerning the avoidance of hazardous behaviour will always be necessary, there is a need to clarify what these messages should consist of and how best to deliver the combination of personal development and effective learning of knowledge and skills to ensure personal competence in the face of hazards such as alcohol and other drugs, as well as the many other potentially hazardous activities.

Educational interventions aimed at developing preference for healthy lifestyle choices in relation to smoking, drinking and drug use require to engage the whole person within the context of the whole school. The scale of this task for educationists should not be underestimated, particularly where schools draw their pupils from communities which have a range of negative health practices embedded in the local culture. To overcome such obstacles it is all the more essential to reassert the role of the individual in his or her own development. Issues of choice and motivation have to be taken into account in drug education programmes which also pay heed to the dynamic and reciprocal relationship between individuals and peers.

NOTE

[1] The importance of the concept of peer preference as opposed to peer pressure was highlighted in a study of health promotion in schools funded by The Portman Group and carried out by the authors.

6

RESPONSES TO AGGRESSION

RESPONSES TO AGGRESSION: WHAT ARE THE CHOICES?

Faced with aggressive young people there are certain steps that can be taken to minimize the potential for matters to become even more problematic. Coping with aggression can require responses at different levels, involving individual responses or responses at an organizational level. The purpose of this chapter is to present some of the key principles underlying successful management of encounters with aggressive people. One of these principles is that in many such encounters there are things that the aggressor's target can do to minimize the potential for aggression to escalate. In addition, we shall discuss some of the lessons learned from a recent successful initiative at an organizational level. This involved a problem of disorder amongst young people who were making life difficult on a Scottish branch line of the rail network, where matters had deteriorated to the extent that staff were in constant fear of aggression and violence.

Men and women of all ages can be subject to fears about being confronted by violence, and understandably so. Particularly vulnerable, it seems, are women – with the fear of sexual assault – and older people being terrorized by young hooligans. In fact, most at risk are young males both as perpetrators and victims. It is widely accepted by experts in the field of aggression and violence that the fear of being a victim often exceeds the actual risk in terms of prevalence across the population. Of course, the prevalence of violent incidents varies depending on where you live, where you go, the type of social activities that you take part in, and the time of day that you visit places of social activity.

One of the key themes of this chapter is that when responding to aggression it can be a matter of choice as to the type of influence you want to have on a difficult situation. This idea of choice is not meant to refer to choice in terms of the social activities that people prefer, though it is obvious that if you choose to visit pubs with a reputation for trouble then you are more at risk than if you choose to spend your leisure time hill-walking in remote areas. So far, so obvious. And the logical conclusion of that approach would be that we would all lock ourselves in our houses when not at work, and never visit any public places. In the real world anyone might, and many do, encounter difficult or aggressive people. This will be especially true for those who work in public or commercial organizations where professional–client contact can entail dealing with people who behave aggressively. Given this likelihood there is a choice to make in the manner of response. Certain responses will be more likely to make matters worse, while other responses will minimize aggression and any potential for violence. What is being suggested here is that there can be an element of control available to the target of aggression in some cases. Before discussing how to respond to aggressive people, including aggressive and drunk people, it would be helpful to clarify which type of incident is amenable to the concept of control by the target.

Different types of aggressive encounters

In general terms the worst type of incident to encounter is where someone has a clear and premeditated plan of attack, for whatever reason, such as revenge or robbery. In these cases there is little that can be done to avoid a dangerous confrontation and the best advice in such circumstances is to run away if at all possible. However, in some cases there will be no opportunity to run away and the victim will be attacked, which might involve fighting back or attempting to defend yourself in some other way. Taking instruction in self-defence techniques is growing in popularity for many individuals and workers who are in high-risk jobs. However, it is not within the scope of this book to go into self-defence techniques. Nonetheless, it is worth pointing out that all employers are legally responsible for providing safe working environments for their employees. In many cases employers fulfil their obligation to protect staff under Health and Safety legislation by providing training, depending on the level of risk involved: in self-defence where the risk is high, in risk-minimization for those at risk of robbery, or training in interpersonal skills and aggression management. The remainder of this chapter has particular relevance for people in occupations that bring them into contact with young people who may be aggressive and/or drunk, such as youth work, social work and teaching, amongst others.

Notwithstanding the comments above about being confronted with someone who has a clear and premeditated plan to carry out an attack, it should be stressed that such encounters represent the minority of cases. Most incidents are less serious, involving aggression from people who have become angry about something but with no premeditation or plan to cause harm. Nonetheless they may have the potential to become more aggressive than they are already. Such incidents need not necessarily become so aggressively charged that violence ensues and it is possible to describe such incidents as 'manageable'. The point is that most encounters with difficult or aggressive individuals can be resolved at least to the extent that the potential for violence is not realized. *This point cannot be stressed enough*. The choice of which direction the encounter takes can lie in the hands of the person on the receiving end of the initial aggression. The initiative may have been taken by the perpetrator, but the choice of response can often lie with the target of aggression. The nature of the target's response will play a very large part in determining the outcome, which could be to precipitate the perpetrator's potential for violence, or it could be to draw the aggressor towards a non-violent conclusion. A successful outcome does not have to be one where the aggressor sees the folly of his or her ways, offers profuse apologies and goes away resolving never to be so stupid again. Far from it: a successful outcome may simply be the perpetrator not becoming any more aggressive than he or she is already. Unless the victim relishes the thought of tackling the aggressor with aggression in turn it should be obvious that to avoid further aggression and violence is a successful result in itself.

The direction that difficult encounters take often depends on the attitude of the person on the receiving end. If the target person has the attitude that nobody should speak or act like that towards him or her and responds in kind, then almost certainly the situation will develop where only might will prevail. This may be appropriate in some circumstances, for instance if the target has the personal strength and skills to engage successfully in a physically violent response and if such actions are morally justified. The intention here is not to discuss the morality of aggressive or violent self-defence. Rather, the perspective adopted here is essentially a pragmatic one, and one which applies in most circumstances of personal threat. This pragmatic philosophy is based on the need to ensure personal safety, to avoid unnecessary conflict and to prevent matters from worsening to the extent that less serious encounters escalate into more serious ones which might result in revenge attacks or other unpleasant knock-on effects.

Dealing with aggression

It is neither possible nor appropriate to provide a simple behavioural blueprint for the containment or management of an aggressive person, for at least two reasons. First, there are considerable differences in personal styles across a range of communication modes, including body language, 'presence', or the impression formed by the other person, and in the extent to which people are verbally agile and can talk their way out of difficulty. Second, dealing with an aggressive person does not entail the deployment of a simple, inflexible set of gestures that everyone can use in the same way, or saying something like 'Calm down'. In a confrontation, for example, people swear or act aggressively as part of their strategy to dominate in the encounter. By showing that swearing and being intemperate is working, is annoying the target, perpetrators will realize that they have chosen an effective strategy. They have been rewarded for its use, and appeal to some sort of social or moral propriety is irrelevant. What is required is a response strategy that builds on what is known about the likely state of an angry and aggressive person. Such a strategy will involve responses that make the person less aroused and/or less frustrated.

Arousal and aggression

We noted in an earlier chapter the importance of the state of arousal in aggression, particularly in explaining how frustration can be a precursor of aggression. Frustration gives rise to a state of arousal which may lead to aggression – which also means that it may not. To understand how arousal can give rise to apparently contradictory behaviours – behaving aggressively or non-aggressively – it is important to look at a classic theory of emotion formulated in the 1960s (Schachter and Singer, 1962; Schachter, 1964). In this theory the state of arousal and the individual's cognitions (thoughts) combine to produce an emotional state. So when someone experiences an emotion-generating situation he or she first of all experiences non-specific physiological arousal. It is what happens next that defines the subjective experience of the arousal state. Arousal is heightened activity in the autonomic nervous system (ANS) and the physiological systems activated by the ANS, such as those systems that require to be in a high state of preparedness to fight or to run away ('fight or flight'). This manifests in increased heart rate, faster respiration, and a subjective experience of agitation or displeasure. If there are cues available to the aroused person which explain the state of arousal, such as the presence of someone or something which has provoked the arousal, then the aroused state will be explicable in these terms. In most cases an aroused person has been provoked by another person or by a situation which provides an obvious explanation for the state of arousal, which will result in feelings of anger towards the source of the provocation.

Schachter and Singer demonstrated their theory with an experiment that involved giving subjects an injection, ostensibly to test the effects of vitamins on vision. Of those subjects who were given adrenalin half were told they would experience the symptoms of arousal as a result of the injection and the other half were not told anything. Subsequently subjects were placed in a room where they completed some questionnaires. Someone who appeared to be another subject joined each subject in a room where they were told to wait for a while and complete some questionnaires. This other person, a confederate of the experimenter, became angry at the nature of the questionnaire and then tore it up before storming out of the room. Those subjects who were not told about the effects of the injection interpreted their state of arousal as a state of anger or irritation, taking their cues from the experimenter's angry confederate. Those subjects who had been told to expect feelings of arousal did not interpret their symptoms in this way, presumably because they could attribute their feelings to the injection. In other words, the thoughts that we have in conjunction with a physiological state of arousal have an important influence on how we react to arousal-generating situations.

Guiding the perpetrator

While the assertion was made earlier that there is no simple way of behaving that is guaranteed to calm an angry person down, it is still possible to identify a number of key factors in the successful management of aggression. It is best to conceive of these factors as behavioural strategies which can guide the perpetrator in the direction that you want him or her to go. One of the underlying problems to take into account when dealing with an angry person is that he or she is aroused (influenced by secretion of adrenalin which prepares the body for fighting or fleeing). It is essential that the perpetrator is guided by the other person in a direction that will lower this state of arousal, for at least two reasons. First, lowering the state of arousal will in itself lessen the likelihood of physical attack. Second, while people are emotionally aroused there is a greater chance of their misconstruing cues and lashing out. When a perpetrator is in this state of arousal there is a very real possibility of violence, which may only be avoided by behaviour that leads the perpetrator in the direction that will dissipate the state of arousal. Moreover, it is possible to guide aggressive persons in this desired direction without their being aware that they are doing what you want them to do, and doing so by means other than telling them to calm down. Sometimes telling an aggressive person to calm down appears to be a successful response, but this will only work with people who are the least likely to become violent anyway. With potentially violent people telling them to calm down can have quite the opposite effect. In other words, with those aggressive people most likely to attack it is all the more important to use appropriate verbal and non-verbal behaviour.

Anyone confronted with an angry and aggressive individual is likely to experience arousal themselves: heart rate will increase, respiration will increase, and there may be a desire to lash out, to hurt the perpetrator, and/or there may be the experience of fear and the desire to escape. In such personal circumstances it becomes more difficult to act calmly and to respond with the controlled and measured responses necessary to guide the perpetrator in the direction required. There is no easy answer or magic solution to this, except to say that people who are experienced in handling aggression learn to minimize the fight-or-flight response, primarily because they have learned to manage such encounters and have gained confidence in their ability to avoid further trouble.

We do not have to respond in any particular way unless we choose to do so. Explanations such as 'I did it because that is just the way I am' should not be taken as reflecting an actual *inability to act in any other way*. For the vast majority of people, excluding the very small percentage who have severe personality disorders, flexibility in behaviour is perfectly normal. Behavioural inflexibility derives from motivation rather than genetic or physiological determinants. When people give such explanations of inflexibility they are saying that they want to be seen as someone who has a personal code that precludes any other reaction. In other words, that is the way they *always choose* to react in the circumstances. While we all experience agitation and displeasure when faced with an aggressive person, drunk or not, and we may even experience a desire to lash out at that person, there is nothing inevitable about doing so. Someone who is inflexible in the face of aggression because 'that's the way they are' is someone whose personal code insists that they are never slighted and that they give as good as they get. When faced with an aggressive person they will be aggressive in reply, matching or exceeding the level of aggression presented to them. If, in turn, the original perpetrator of the aggression responds with a higher level of aggression the target will also escalate, giving rise to a cycle of aggression that increases the likelihood of violence and physical assault. For such people, to choose behaviours other than their usual repertoire would involve rethinking their attitudes to themselves and the image that they present to others.

RESPONSES TO AGGRESSION: WHAT BEHAVIOURS TO CHOOSE?

In the first part of this chapter we looked at some of the main issues to take into account when choosing how to respond to aggression from another person. While the choice of appropriate behaviour is critical to the outcome of aggressive encounters, it is also the case that the ease with which people can respond appropriately depends on their confidence in doing so, confidence which usually comes from experience of success in managing outcomes in aggressive situations. What aspects of verbal and non-verbal behaviour make the difference between successful and unsuccessful outcomes?

The responses required when faced with someone both aggressive and intoxicated are the same as when faced with someone who is aggressive but sober. In fact, there is even greater need for responses that unambiguously communicate non-aggression to intoxicated persons as their ability to process multiple stimuli or cues simultaneously will be impaired. Which means that there is a greater chance of their misinterpreting the verbal and non-verbal cues presented to them.

How not to react

Aggression is out. So is being over-compliant. If you respond with aggression it will make matters worse. If you are overly compliant you may also make yourself more of a target. This is the case both at the level of less serious encounters, where over-compliance may encourage the perpetrator to continue being aggressive through a sense of reward, and at the level of the extremely dangerous hostage situation, where over-compliance has been recognized as leading to extreme punishment by perpetrators (Fuselier, 1991). Successful approaches when dealing with aggressive and intoxicated people are based on the following:

- Self-monitoring.
- De-personalizing the encounter.
- Using appropriate body language: e.g. avoiding aggressive or anxious appearance, pointing, clenching fists or teeth; sudden movements; invasion of personal space; aggressive eye contact.

In broad terms it is important to be neither belligerent nor dismissive. What is said, how it is said, and body language must not be perceived as aggressive. To do this will involve rejection of the use of threats, sarcasm, a dismissive attitude or manner, and avoiding being side-tracked by the manner of expression such as swearing. It will involve recognizing the other person's point of view, or appearing to at least. So, for example, it would help to defuse the situation if an emotionally neutral and assertive manner of speaking is adopted when saying things such as:

- 'If I was in your situation I would be upset too.'
- 'Look at it from my point of view – my hands are tied.'

- 'I'll find out what can be done and let you know.'

However, the point about such quotes is not to suggest that difficult and aggressive people will be mollified by a few simple words; it is what is conveyed that is crucial. There are many ways of communicating that an aggressive outcome is not wanted. If the angry person feels that they are being taken seriously he or she will be more likely to calm down. Achieving an outcome in which perpetrators feel they are getting something out of it, even if that something is very small in material terms, can ameliorate any frustration underlying perpetrators' aggression.

Self-monitoring and de-personalization

People who are good at coping with aggressive drunks are able to monitor the impact of what they are saying and doing on the other person. If something is said or done that has the effect of making the perpetrator more aggressive, they will note it and ensure it is not repeated. Aggressive people will have their own good reasons for being angry and aggressive, or at least what they think are good reasons. One way to take some heat out of a difficult situation is to de-personalize the encounter. By communicating to the perpetrator that you are not responsible for the aggressor's failure to achieve his or her goal, much of the aggression will be deflected. Blame the situation: 'Look, there is a problem here ... not you ... but the situation is not under my control ... All I can do is ... '

A reasonably convincing explanation in terms of the constraints of circumstances is more effective than an explanation in terms of one person's personal demands of the other person. It is not surprising that people who have good verbal skills and can present what is essentially the same argument in a variety of forms tend to be good at coping with aggressive people. The key point here is to avoid being perceived as the impediment: and this can be done by developing an ability to be verbally agile under pressure.

Body language

Verbal communication with aggressive people, particularly when they are intoxicated, will be all the more effective when the content of speech is supported by body language that signals non-aggression. An intoxicated person has a narrowed ability to attend to a range of cues simultaneously and this requires that the clearest possible cues are presented non-verbally. With a sober person non-verbal communication is more powerful than verbal communication, as these cues can indicate that there is no aggressive intent. *This is all the more important with an intoxicated person.*

Saying something (verbally) that could be frustrating for the aggressor can be softened, presented in the context of body language which says 'This is not a threat . . . This person does not intend any harm.' For example, using open gestures such as arms pointing roughly downwards with the hands held wide of the body and palms open and facing the other person. The use of such open gestures softens the negative verbal message. Even in the absence of a verbal message, such a gesture powerfully communicates non-aggressive intent. Contrast this with pointing, or clenching fists, which powerfully communicate aggressive feelings if not intent.

Avoid staring at the perpetrator's eyes. Think of the normal pattern of eye contact, where the speaker tends to direct his or her gaze at the object of the communication intermittently, as if checking that the other person is still paying attention to what the speaker is saying, while the listener tends to look more frequently and for longer periods at the eyes of the speaker. Disrupting this 'normal' pattern of eye contact can signal intentions that may not even be present, or that may be unhelpful under the circumstances. Holding the perpetrator's gaze will almost certainly be interpreted as aggressive intent.

Avoid sudden movements which could suggest that a physical assault was under way and avoid being too close to the perpetrator. Perhaps less intuitively obvious is to avoid looking anxious, as there are certain similarities between anxious faces and aggressive faces. This can be especially true when people are intoxicated as they are more likely to make mistakes and misinterpret anxiety as aggression.

RESPONSES TO AGGRESSION: A CASE STUDY

In the preceding pages we looked at how individuals should respond when faced with an aggressive person, with the focus on interpersonal skills. However, sometimes an aggressive encounter is part of a wider problem of ongoing disorder associated with a particular place or activity. The potential for violence at a wide range of public events is recognized by the authorities who police football matches and other such gatherings of people not always well disposed to each other. The threat of arrest often prevents violence from erupting, or displaces it to another locality. On other occasions, however, the option of high-profile policing is limited or simply not practicable. Sometimes it is essential for people in the front line not only to deploy the behavioural skills described above, but also to be part of a co-ordinated approach within which different levels of an organization respond in a coherent manner to problems of disorder. One such problem of disorder was faced by staff on a rail service which linked a number of small towns on a branch line near Glasgow.

Initial reports from British Transport Police and ScotRail indicated that there was particular concern about groups of adolescents being disruptive, being aggressive and even threatening violence. There were also reports of drunkenness. There was concern in general about anti-social behaviour being widespread amongst the passengers using this line. Matters had reached a stage where staff were fearful, revenue was not being collected, and evening trains were staffed by additional personnel. Trains were monitored by plain-clothes policemen and shadowed by police vans to provide fast response to incidents. The situation was such that matters could not continue given the disruption to non-problem passengers, the stress to staff, and the dedication of police resources to the detriment of other responsibilities. Psychologists were brought in to advise on how to return the line to normal. An assessment of the problem was carried out over a period of a month, with various aspects of the situation monitored including behaviour on the trains, in local bars or other areas where young people congregated such as public parks at night. Observation was carried out by a team of researchers without revealing the purpose of their presence to anyone on the trains or in any of the towns where the troublesome passengers were thought to originate from.

The rail line concerned served small towns with moderately high levels of deprivation and there was a general lack of recreational facilities for younger people. Apart from several public houses and carry-out food facilities there were no centres of social activity for younger people, particularly people who were not old enough to go to local bars. The outcome of these observations included development of a strategy for normalization, involving individual and corporate responses (Davies and Coggans, 1991b).

The scale of the problem

Staff reported to the research team that a number of unpleasant incidents had taken place, with staff being threatened with knives, incidents of vandalism on the train, and trains being stoned. There was fear that trains might be deliberately stopped by shorting out the power lines or blocking the track, and sets subsequently 'ambushed'. There was widespread belief among personnel that something unusual was happening, which had given rise to the threat to withdraw staff from the line. All of which had resulted in volunteer crews 'riding shotgun' with additional presence in the form of rail inspectors, plain-clothes and uniformed police. There was clearly a need to go beyond the largely impressionistic and stereotypical picture that had developed of the problems on the line and to identify the underlying causes.

It became apparent from observation that in some respects the problem was not as bad as had been anticipated from first soundings. Some preconceptions were misplaced and in large part the line was free of major incidents. Some passengers themselves reported that it was possible to travel the branch line with no sense of personal threat. However, despite the perception of the problem having become greater than the incidence of actual violence, there were matters that required to be tackled. One consequence of the problem existing, in part, at the level of perception was that whenever incidents did occur they tended to assume a significance that confirmed expectations of disruption.

Solving the problem

Having assessed the nature and scale of the problem for rail staff it remained to develop their skills and willingness to tackle incidents effectively. A key feature of the problem was that relationships between staff and passengers had developed in a very negative way and staff needed to develop both their interpersonal skills and their confidence to rebuild relationships on the line. Over a period of time, probably even a number of years, relationships between staff and passengers had deteriorated. Many passengers showed no respect for rail staff and some went out of their way to cause disruption. For their part, staff felt persecuted and respect for passengers had diminished. A number of passengers and staff were almost engaged in a self-perpetuating battle of wits and worse. Staff expected problems and their anxiety gave every minor problem a significance far beyond the actual level of difficulty involved. Troublesome passengers had reached the stage of believing that it was almost required of them that they should cause problems for the rail staff.

The return to normal operation and normal relationships was achieved by a number of means within a co-ordinated strategy, including training for staff in aggression-management skills and by means of a progressive strategy for establishing more positive relations with difficult passengers, involving progressive reduction in the amount of additional staff/police involvement on the line. The high level of additional staff presence was progressively reduced to remove the sense of abnormality from the perspective of passengers, which itself could have influenced expectations of aggression from their side of the equation (there were proud reports from young passengers that 'all this is just for us'), and to re-establish normal rail staff as being in charge. This required that staff developed a higher profile on the trains, spending more time with passengers where appropriate and attempting always to be in the vicinity of those who appeared to have the potential to be high-spirited or troublesome. Which simply means that staff had to be prepared to engage passengers and situations, rather than saying little or nothing and moving away in the hope that the situation would sort itself out. It also required that staff handled every potentially difficult encounter in ways that would minimize rather than exacerbate aggression.

The success of the strategy rested primarily on the willingness of staff to engage passengers and build relationships with them, and their use of aggression-management techniques where necessary. It would be wrong to give the impression that everything is perfect now on the line in question. But it is true to say that staff feel a great deal more comfortable, they feel less threatened and they report that there are fewer problems to cope with. The essential point is that problems of disorder and aggression can be tackled.

CHAPTER SUMMARY

In this chapter we discussed the key principles of aggression with particular regard to intoxication and how best to react if having to deal with a potentially violent individual. Just as situations will vary, so will the specific behaviours to be deployed by anyone trying to placate a drunk and aggressive person. Nonetheless, there are aspects of response that can be effective in guiding the perpetrator in the direction of being less aroused and aggressive.

We have also looked at a particular case history where aggressive incidents were part of a deteriorating problem of public disorder on public transport. Again this situation was retrievable, utilizing the skills of staff and building their confidence to tackle the problem.

7
CONCLUSIONS

ISSUES AND INTERVENTIONS

In the preceding chapters we looked at a number of the main issues surrounding alcohol and disorder among young people. In so doing we recognized that alcohol is a central feature of young people's lives. The growing normalization of illicit drug use also serves to make this centrality of alcohol use all the less remarkable. Clearly, alcohol use *per se* need not be a problem, even for young people. Problems arise from over-indulgence either in terms of too much alcohol during any one drinking session, or from too frequent consumption. Aggression and violence is also recognized as a problem, if not quite on the scale implied by some of the lurid accounts presented by the more irresponsible sections of the media. To the extent that trends are discernible it appears that we are more rather than less likely to experience at least the same levels of alcohol-related disorder in the future, if not higher levels.

It has also been shown how some of the more popular explanations for certain forms of delinquency, and not simply popular in the sense of only being given credence by lay people, are over-simplifications or even misinterpretations. Given that educational interventions are often based on inadequate understanding of the dynamics of peer relations some reappraisal of responses is indicated. Some people will take the view that redefining peer pressure in terms of peer preference relates primarily to the area of substance misuse. This would be a mistake. It is most unlikely that the dynamics of illicit drug use are so very different from the dynamics of other behaviours such as drinking, rowdiness and aggression.

The importance of the peer preference redefinition is that this would permit and facilitate interventions that are more likely to be effective. Barely disguised 'say no' messages must surely be consigned to history (Coggans *et al.*, 1991b). There is growing interest in peer education and any interventions based on this approach must take into account the true nature of the relationships between individuals and peers. A key assumption in peer education is that there is a greater empathy between the target group and peer educators than would be the case with older educators. The efficacy of such programmes will relate more to peer-preference models rather than simplistic peer-pressure models.

Redefinition of peer pressure as peer preference is not the same as saying that peer factors do not operate. The question arises as to what influences the development of differential patterns of peer preference. This entails assessing the formative influences on children prior to the ages at which they form associations with like-minded peers. While there is still the issue of the dynamics of attitude and behaviour reinforcement within peer networks, this is not the same as some of the less sophisticated definitions of peer pressure. What leads young people to develop interest in alcohol and drugs? What leads them to develop aggressive patterns of responses?

We have seen that a variety of socio-economic and cultural factors are related to offending; and we have seen how social and situational factors influence aggressiveness. In particular it was shown that aggression in individual encounters can be influenced by subtle social cues as well as the more overt cues and facilitators of aggression. Other evidence was brought in from an organizational perspective supporting the view that patterns of disorder and aggression can be greatly improved, for example on public transport. Clearly there are also more intractable problems which require more fundamental remedies. From several practical points of view massive social engineering is unlikely, to say the least, and it is not the intention here to discuss the political or economic implications of any level of intervention, though clearly there are many of significance.

Nonetheless, there are lessons to be learned from the evidence reviewed here, which apply at the individual level, at the level of organizations, and on a wider societal level.

Culture of aggression

In a previous chapter we touched on the subject of social and cultural influences on aggression; in particular how young people are influenced by those within their immediate social network. Using the term micro-culture to describe the proximal social influences, it was suggested that exposure to an ethos or climate of aggressiveness would make it more likely that young people will learn to behave aggressively. The findings of experimental work and other evidence reviewed in Chapter 4 support this view. In the light of these findings it is important to look more closely at the ways in which this would influence a young person's behavioural development.

The nature of the aggression-priming effect, found to be so important in the experimental setting, derives from the establishment of a negative attitude towards someone. This gave rise to an implicit expectation or acceptance of aggressiveness towards the target of this negative attitude. It is reasonable therefore to conclude that individuals exposed to a social setting which is characterized by an ethos of negative attitudes towards others would themselves tend to behave aggressively towards the target. While there are many ways in which this can happen, of particular interest is the situation that reinforces the development of an aggressive pattern of behaviour, rather than the occasional or untypical aggressive incident.

The implications of this for parents are that it is important that they should at all times ensure that the climate within the family is not one of aggressive negativity towards others. Where it is, and where any aggressiveness on the part of children is rewarded or encouraged, there is a greater likelihood of aggressiveness becoming part of the typical repertoire of behaviour. This will make it all the more likely that aggression becomes the response of first preference. Once established, such a pattern of behaviour will be more difficult to change. However, it is not the intention to suggest that parents are always and wholly to blame either for the personalities of their children or for their subsequent deeds as adults. Genetic inheritance makes an important contribution. For example, it has been shown that certain characteristics in recently born children are correlated with aggression and irritability in later life. These characteristics include irregularity in eating and sleeping patterns, poor adaptability to new situations, and negative mood (Thomas and Chess, 1977).

Simple solutions fail to address underlying causes

'At present we are presented with the rather neat combination of video nasties causing crime and regular television viewing causing fear [of violent crime]. Such a simple formula simply takes the focus away from the structural problems which engender crime and which in turn give rise to, if not fear, anger and dismay amongst a large proportion of the population.'

(Professor Jock Young, Head of Centre for Criminology, Middlesex University, in a letter to the *Guardian*, 8 June 1994)

Nonetheless, the process of socialization has been recognized as an important influence in its own right. Where children are socialized in an atmosphere of aggressiveness we should not be surprised when such children grow into aggressive adults. While some children may become withdrawn and anxious as a consequence of exposure to family-centred aggression others will learn that aggression is a 'normal' way of life and incorporate aggressiveness into their repertoire of responses. Of course aggressiveness takes many forms within the family, including aggressiveness towards children by parents. A recent study by Wolff (1985) reported that a number of family characteristics were related to aggressiveness in children, including irritable parents, marital discord, absent fathers, divorce and large family size. While one or more of these factors are not sufficient in themselves to give rise to aggressiveness in a child, these are recurring themes and patterns within the micro-culture of aggressive children. Without wishing to go beyond the data concerned, it is possible to speculate that the difference between families which are the same in terms of structural disturbance, such as divorce or parental absence, but which differ in the presence or absence of aggressive children, may well be the presence or absence respectively of an ethos of negativity and aggressiveness. A word of caution though: it is important to allow for the possibility that family discord could be the result of difficult and aggressive children, rather than the other way round. That is, the causal direction may not always be from the parents to the children (Pearce, 1992). The point at issue here is that, while it is possible to point to genetic and other influences over which parents may not have control, there is still a need for parents to ensure that aggressiveness is not part of the cultural environment.

The origins of dysfunctional behaviour, including alcohol and drug misuse, amongst young people stem in large part from early experience within the family setting, where early socialization has an important influence on development of problem behaviours. A recent review and meta-analysis of thirty published research reports, which addressed the family-behaviour variables related to children's drinking, demonstrated the importance of certain variables; namely, support, control and family cohesion (Foxcroft and Lowe, 1991). Children whose parents fail to provide adequate support, appropriate forms of control and family cohesion are at risk of developing problems of alcohol misuse.

There is also evidence that family discord is a principal source of childhood problems among children of problem drinkers. For example, it has been shown that children of problem drinkers experience a range of negative childhood traumas, including less cohesive and stable relationships, negative and violent family relationships, and separation between family and outside relationships (Velleman and Orford, 1993).

The thrust of these bodies of research is that early social influences on children are critical factors in the development of dysfunctional attitudes and behaviours. Thus, for example, it is important to identify dysfunctional families before children are negatively influenced by discordant family environment. In many cases this will involve intervention before children reach the age at which peer assortment results in the formation of peer groups which provide support for problem behaviours. In other words, supportive intervention at an early age has the potential to be more effective than (a) reactive intervention once problem behaviours have developed, or (b) educational interventions during adolescence. Early interventions should address the psychological and socialization factors that predispose children to develop problem behaviours.

To a large extent support services have focused on the needs of the presenting adults in isolation from their families. There is a need to develop more supportive intervention and input from a family and child-centred perspective. Where children are raised in dysfunctional families which are not in contact with helping agencies, identification and assessment for possible intervention is difficult, though such children will often present problems in school or in later years. In those instances where parents with alcohol problems, for example, are in contact with helping agencies the possibility clearly exists that their children may also be experiencing problems. Where one or more family members are in contact with helping agencies the opportunity exists to develop early interventions with the aim of countering and/or resolving negative socialization before children manifest problems in later years.

At a recent conference on alcohol and crime a former Head of the Home Office Research and Planning Unit made a coherent and convincing case for the importance of culture, normative factors and the need for positive early influences to offset the problems of deprivation and failure to adopt positive cultural influences on drinking patterns (Tuck, 1993). The liberty is taken here of recounting the key elements of Tuck's argument. Citing evidence from the UK, Ireland and other European member states, it was argued that the roots of heavy drinking, criminality and aggressiveness were to be found in large part in failures of parenting, being taken into care (and presumably the failure of caring institutions to redress the negative influences already experienced, as well as perhaps having a negative impact themselves), and the development of lawlessness through failure to absorb the bases of positive attitudes to more conventional norms (Marsh and Kibby, 1992; O'Connor, 1978; Walmsley, 1992).

The point was made earlier that when the micro-culture of the proximal social environment and that of the wider macro-culture is consistent, inasmuch as they both contain elements of negativity and aggressiveness, there is a greater likelihood of the child becoming aggressive. One example of how this might work can be inferred from a recent study that showed how school characteristics are related to problems of aggression amongst pupils (Besag, 1989). Of particular note are characteristics such as low staff morale, unclear standards of expected behaviour, inconsistency in discipline, and a failure to communicate to pupils the importance of the needs of individuals. The same caveat that applies to correlations of family characteristics with aggression in children also applies to correlations of school characteristics with aggressive pupils. That is, it may be that in some cases low staff morale could be the effect of aggressive pupils rather than the cause. Nonetheless, schools are professional organizations which can respond effectively to disruptive young people. Schools that have more positive characteristics have a big enough job to cope with children from families where the social environment is conducive to the development of aggressiveness. Where both the family and the school exhibit these risk factors the problem is compounded. There is then little to counterbalance the influence of the negative micro-culture.

A leading researcher in the field of aggression and bullying in children has pointed to the ways of relating and attitudes to aggression within families that are risk factors in the predisposition to aggression in children (Olweus, 1984). Parents who rely on aggressive physical punishment and aggressive emotions as means of control are more likely to foster aggressiveness in their children. So also are parents who fail to promote warmth and involvement in their relations with their children, or who have an acceptance of aggression and fail to set limits on aggressiveness in their children. Conceptually these characteristics are identical with the nature of the aggression-priming effect used in the alcohol and aggression experiment described in an earlier chapter. Given the power of this factor to influence aggressiveness on an isolated occasion, the power that such micro-cultural features have when present on a regular basis must be considerable.

Much of the foregoing has underlined the responsibilities of parents in establishing the right sort of family ethos. In many ways the parents most receptive to this message will be the ones who are most likely to respond in an appropriate manner, and may well have already established such an atmosphere. Parents who are themselves emotionally damaged and exhibit aggression-priming characteristics will probably be the least receptive and least likely to change their behaviour. While this is almost certainly a truism, it bears repeating because of the need to recognize the importance of the family in perpetuating aggressiveness in our society. Recent longitudinal research provides evidence for the importance of avoiding the early establishment of aggressiveness. While the researchers found that heavy drinking was not a predictor of aggressiveness, they also found that aggressiveness at the age of 7 years was a predictor of heavy drinking in later life (White *et al.*, 1992). On the basis of these data it can be argued that development of aggressive traits is a risk factor for heavy drinking, which is a reversal of popular perceptions of the relationship between alcohol and aggression.

Recognizing parents' responsibility and the power of their influence in the perpetuation of aggression is a necessary precursor to the development of strategies and interventions designed to shift social and family mores in the direction of lowered aggressiveness. The problem that the reader will already have identified is the problem of how to intervene and, perhaps more important, is there an ethical issue attendant upon such interventions? It is easy to sympathize with desires for a less aggressive society, but more difficult to establish mechanisms for intervention consistent with an individual's right to freedom from overweening intervention by agents of social control. However, the matter requires more than hand-wringing and the objective is not only worthy but of central importance both for the maintenance of low-aggression societies and for the prevention of the development of high-aggression societies. As a society we have no compunction about direct interventions in the affairs of families and individuals for behaviours such as illicit drug use, even where the harm associated with such behaviour is minimal or non-existent by any objective psychological or physiological indices. The issue is not one of extending such treatment, whether it is at the hands of the criminal justice system or via the 'caring' services; it is to recognize that we can and do sanction intervention in family matters when we want to. While we would have to balance costs and benefits – more harm than good might be done by intervening in certain circumstances, or by the manner of intervention – the rights of those who will suffer what can be termed preventable aggression and violence dictate that some sort of intervention should be considered where aggression is promoted. It is not being suggested that all manifestations of aggression be made sanctionable in the way that criminal offences are, as there is often a *higher* cost to be paid by society by criminalization of certain activities than the costs of the behaviours themselves. But we do need to move towards social agencies with responsibilities for care and welfare of children to be able to counteract the power of aggressive micro-cultures. Pie in the sky it may seem, but defeatism is not one of the more useful human characteristics.

It is interesting to note in this context that what we like to think of as caring professions/interventions have themselves been guilty of mistakes and harm. This is not a reference to the more extreme and high profile interventions responsible for disrupting children's lives to their detriment (remember the issue of satanic child sex abuse). Rather it is a reference to the increasing recognition in some quarters that what passes as care can sometimes hide 'a strong vein of aggression and dislike' (Mugford, 1994). While such sentiments may not be typical, it can be argued that as a society we do little to address underlying causes of many social problems. There are a number of educational programmes for young offenders which aim to help them reappraise their attitudes and behaviour, but success is partial. Once patterns of behaviour and social identities have become established they are relatively difficult to change. Proactive interventions should have the potential to prevent such difficult-to-change behaviours from developing. It is self-evident that many, if not all, of the responses to aggressive and disorderly adolescents tried in the past have not served to lower levels of aggression and violence in society.

SUMMARY

Having reviewed a lot of evidence, a number of general points can be made. Given that much of the discussion has focused on social and cultural factors that encourage aggression and alcohol abuse, it is important to recognize the scale of the problem. There are no quick fixes. Some level of aggression appears to be inevitable and we have to develop ways of controlling and containing that which is inevitable. But we also have to realize that the methods that are used to 'manage' aggression and violence may not always be effective and sometimes can be counter-productive. It is easy to say that prison and detention do not appear to work, and even make things worse if we look at recidivism rates, but the answer to this is not simply to denigrate detention as such. After all there are people for whom segregation from society is the only reasonable strategy. Yet there is clearly a need to reappraise the function of detention and prison. Does the experience of prison encountered by inmates, particularly young offenders, actually serve the needs of those who are supposed to be protected by sending offenders to prison? Which programmes of rehabilitation work and which don't?

We looked at ways in which problems of disorder in public places can be improved by co-ordinated organizational responses. There is also a need to address the issue of support services for the children of people who have drink problems. At the moment the focus is often on problem drinkers and substance-users and fails to address the needs of their families. On a broader front there is a need to ensure that aggression is not promoted and encouraged in the everyday aspects of social functioning. Perhaps we need to reassert the importance of non-aggressive ways of interacting on more occasions than is the case at present.

REFERENCES

Advisory Council on the Misuse of Drugs (ACMD) (1993) *Drug Education in Schools: The Need for a New Impetus.* London: HMSO.

Aitken, P.P. (1978) *Ten-to-Fourteen Year Olds and Alcohol: A Developmental Study in the Central Region of Scotland*. London: HMSO.

Akers, R.L. (1977) *Deviant Behaviour: Social Learning Approach*. Belmont, CA: Wadsworth.

Akers, R.L. and Cochran, J.K. (1985) Adolescent marijuana use: A test of three theories of deviant behaviour. *Deviant Behaviour*, **6**, 323–46.

Akers, R.L., Krohn, M.D., Lanza-Kaduce, L. and Radosevich, M. (1979) Social learning and deviant behaviour: A specific test of a general theory. *American Sociological Review,* **44** (August), 636–55.

Austin, G. (1988) *Prevention Research Update,* no. 1. Portland, OR: Western Center for Drug-Free Schools and Communities.

Bachman, J.G., O'Malley, P.M. and Johnston, L.D. (1984) Drug use among young adults: The impacts of role status and social environment. *Journal of Personality and Social Psychology*, **47**(3), 629–45.

Bagnall, G. (1988) Use of alcohol, tobacco and illicit drugs amongst 13-year-olds in three areas in Britain. *Drug and Alcohol Dependence,* **22**, 241–51.

Bahr, S.J., Hawks, R.D. and Wang, G. (1993) Family and religious influences on adolescent substance abuse. *Youth and Society,* **24**(4), 443–65.

Baldwin, S. (1993) Alcohol education courses for offenders. In J.

Russell (ed.), *Alcohol and Crime: Proceedings of a Mental Health Foundation Conference*. London: Mental Health Foundation.

Bandura, A. (1977) *Social Learning Theory*. Englewood Cliffs, NJ: Prentice-Hall.

Baumrind, D. (1985) Familial antecedents of adolescent drug use: A developmental perspective. In C.L. Jones and R.J. Battjes (eds), *Etiology of Drug Abuse: Implications for Prevention*. Research Monograph 56. Washington, DC: National Institute on Drug Abuse.

Belson, W.A., Millerson, G.L. and Didcott, P.T. (1968) *The Development of a Procedure for Eliciting Information from Boys about the Nature and Extent of Their Stealing*. A report of the Survey Research Centre. London: Survey Research Centre.

Berkowitz, L. (1993) *Aggression: Its Causes, Consequences, and Control*. New York: McGraw-Hill.

Besag, V.E. (1989) *Bullies and Victims in Schools: A Guide to Understanding and Management*. Milton Keynes: Open University Press.

Biddle, B.J., Bank, B.J. and Marlin, M.M. (1980) Parental and peer influence on adolescents. *Social Forces* **58**(4), 1057–79.

Botvin, G.J., Baker, E., Filazzola, A.D. and Botvin, E.M. (1990) A cognitive-behavioral approach to substance abuse prevention: One-year follow-up. *Addictive Behaviors* **15**, 47–63.

Boyatzis, R.E. (1974) The effect of alcohol consumption on the aggressive behaviour of men. *Quarterly Journal of Studies on Alcohol,* **35**, 959–72.

Britt, D.W. and Campbell, E.Q. (1977) Assessing the linkage of norms, environments, and deviance. *Social Forces,* **56**(2), 532–50.

Brook, J.S., Whiteman, M. and Gordon, A.S. (1983) Stages of drug use in adolescence: Personality, peer and family correlates. *Developmental Psychology,* **19**(2), 269–77.

Burgess, R.L. and Akers, R.L. (1966) A differential association-reinforcement theory of criminal behaviour. *Social Problems,* **14**, 128–47.

Bushman, B.J. and Cooper, H.M. (1990) Effects of alcohol on human aggression: An integrative research review. *Psychological Bulletin,* **107**(3), 341–54.

Buss, A.H. (1961) *The Psychology of Aggression*. New York: Wiley.

Coggans, N. and Davies, J.B. (1988) Explanations for heroin use. *Journal of Drug Issues,* **18**(3), 457–65.

Coggans, N., Henderson, M., Shewan, D., Macpherson, S. and McKellar, S. (1994) *Alcohol, Aggression, Personality and Social Context.* Glasgow, University of Strathclyde: Alcohol Education and Research Council.

Coggans, N. and McKellar, S. (1994) Drug use amongst peers: Peer pressure or peer preference? *Drugs Education, Prevention & Policy,* **1**(1), 15–26.

Coggans, N., Shewan, D., Henderson, M. and Davies, J.B. (1991a) *National Evaluation of Drug Education in Scotland*. ISDD Research Monograph 4. London: Institute for the Study of Drug Dependence.

Coggans, N., Shewan, D., Henderson, M. and Davies, J.B. (1991b) The impact of school-based drug education. *British Journal of Addiction,* **86**, 1099–109.

Cohen, J.M. (1977) Sources of peer group homogeneity. *Sociology of Education,* **50**(4) (October), 227–41.

Collins, J.J. (ed.) (1982) *Drinking and Crime.* London: Tavistock Publications.

Currie, C. and Todd, J. (1990) *Health Behaviours of Scottish Schoolchildren:* Report 1: *National and Regional Patterns.* Edinburgh: University of Edinburgh, Research Unit in Health and Behavioural Change.

Davies, J.B. (1992) *The Myth of Addiction*. Reading: Harwood Academic.

Davies, J.B. and Baker, R. (1987) The impact of self-presentation and interviewer bias effects on self-reported heroin use. *British Journal of Addiction,* **82**, 907–12.

Davies, J.B. and Coggans, N. (1991a) *The Facts about Adolescent Drug Abuse*. London: Cassell.

Davies, J.B. and Coggans, N. (1991b) *Disorder on ScotRail: An Evaluation*. Glasgow: ScotRail.

Davies, J.B. and Stacey, B. (1972) *Teenagers and Alcohol: A Developmental Study in Glasgow.* London: HMSO.

Deffenbacher, J.L., Demm, P.M. and Brandon, A.D. (1986) High general anger: Correlates and treatment. *Behaviour Research and Therapy,* **24**, 481–9.

Dielman, T.E., Campanelli, P.C., Shope, J.T. and Butchart, A.T. (1987) Susceptibility of peer pressure, self-esteem and health locus of control as correlates of adolescent substance abuse. *Health Education Quarterly,* **14**(2), 207–21.

Dielman, T.E., Shope, J.T., Butchart, A.T., Campanelli, P.C. and Caspar, R.A. (1989) A covariance structure model test of antecedents of adolescent alcohol misuse and a prevention effort. *Journal of Drug Education,* **19**(4), 337–61.

Dobash, R.E. and Dobash, R.P. (1987) Violence against wives. In J. Orford (ed.), *Coping with Disorder in the Family.* London: Croom Helm.

Doleys, E.J., Otto, J.E., Osborne, F.E., Harris, C.D. and Snyder, D. (1967) Varying amounts of alcohol and personal inventory performance. *Journal of Clinical Psychology,* **23**(4), 484–6.

Dollard, J., Doob, L.W., Miller, N.E., Mowrer, O.H. and Sears, R.R. (1939) *Frustration and Aggression*. New Haven, CT: Yale University Press.

Donovan, J.E. and Jessor, R. (1978) Adolescent problem drinking – Psychosocial correlates in a national sample study. *Journal of Studies in Alcohol,* **39**, 1506–24.

Donovan, J.E. and Jessor, R. (1983) Problem drinking and the dimension of involvement with drugs: A Guttman scalogram analysis of adolescent drug use. *American Journal of Public Health,* **73**, 543–52.

Dorn, N. (1983) *Alcohol, Youth and the State: Drinking Practices, Controls, and Health Education*. London: Croom Helm.

Eagly, A.H. and Steffen, F.J. (1986) Gender and aggressive behaviour: A meta-analytic review of the social psychological literature. *Psychological Bulletin,* **100**, 309–30.

Egeland, B., Jacobvitz, D. and Sroufe, L.A. (1988) Breaking the cycle of abuse. *Child Development,* **59**, 1080–8.

Eisterhold, M.J., Murphy, P., Beneke, W. and Scott, G. (1979) Multiple drug use among high school students. *Psychological Reports,* **44**, 1099–106.

Elder, J.P., Stern, R.A., Anderson, M., Hovell, M.F., Molgaard, C.A. and Seidman, R.L. (1987) Contingency-based strategies for preventing alcohol, drug and tobacco use: Missing or unwanted components of adolescent health promotion? *Education and Treatment of Children,* **10**(1), 33–47.

Endler, N.S. and Magnusson, D. (1976) Towards an interactional psychology of personality. *Psychological Bulletin,* **83**, 956–74.

Fagan, Jeffrey (1990) Intoxication and aggression. In M. Tonry and J.Q. Wilson (eds), *Drugs and Crime*. London: University of Chicago Press Ltd.

Farrington, D.P. (1983) Offending from 10 to 25 years of age. In K. Teilmann van Dusen and S.A. Mednick (eds), *Prospective Studies of Crime and Delinquency*. The Hague: Kluwer Nijhoff.

Farrington, D.P. (1987) Epidemiology. In H.C. Quay (ed.), *Handbook of Juvenile Delinquency*. New York: Wiley.

Feshback, S. (1964) The function of aggression and the regulation of aggressive drive. *Psychological Review,* **71**, 257–72.

Foxcroft, D.R. and Lowe, G. (1991) Adolescent drinking behaviour and family socialisation factors: A meta analysis. *Journal of Adolescence,* **14**, 255–73.

Fuselier, G.D. (1991) Hostage negotiation: Issues and applications. In R. Gal and A.D. Mangeldorff (eds), *Handbook of Military Psychology*. Chichester: Wiley.

Gaffney, L.R. and McFall, R.M. (1981) A comparison of social skills in delinquent and non-delinquent adolescent girls using behavioural role-play inventory. *Journal of Consulting and Clinical Psychology,* **49**, 959–67.

Geen, R.G. (1990) *Human Aggression*. Milton Keynes: Open University Press.

Goddard, E. (1991) *Drinking in England and Wales in the Late 1980s*. London: HMSO.

Hamburg, D.A. (1992) *Children of Urban Poverty: Approaches to a Critical American Problem*. New York: Carnegie Corporation of New York.

Hammersley, R., Forsyth, A., Morrison, V. and Davies, J.B. (1989) The relationship between crime and opioid use. *British Journal of Addiction,* **84**, 1029–43.

Hammersley, R., Morrison, V., Davies, J., Forsyth, A. (1988) *Heroin Use and Crime*. Report to the Scottish Home and Health Department.

Hartford, T.C. and Spiegler, D.L. (1983) Developmental trends of adolescent drinking. *The Journal of Studies on Alcohol,* **44**(1).

Hawker, A. (1978) *Adolescents and Alcohol*. London: Edsall.

Hays, R.D., Stacy, A.W. and Dimatteo, M.D. (1987) Problem behavior theory and adolescent alcohol use. *Addictive Behaviors,* **12**, 189–93.

Hewstone, M. (ed.) (1983) *Attribution Theory: Social and Functional Extensions*. Oxford: Blackwell.

Home Office Statistical Bulletin (1993a) *Cautions, Court Proceedings and Sentencing (England and Wales 1992)*. Issue 24/93. London: Government Statistical Service.

Home Office Statistical Bulletin (1993b) *Offences of Drunkenness (England and Wales 1991)*. Issue 20/93. London: Government Statistical Service.

Huba, G. and Bentler, P.M. (1982) A developmental theory of drug use: Derivation and assessment of a causal modelling approach. In P.B. Baltes and O.G. Brim (eds), *Life-Span Development and Behavior*, Vol. 4, 147–203. New York: Academic Press.

Huba, G., Wingard, J. and Bentler, P. (1980) Framework for an interactive theory of drug use. In D.J. Lettieri, M. Sayers and H.W. Pearson (eds), *Theories on Drug Abuse*. Rockville: National Institute on Drug Abuse.

Huntly, M.S. (1973) Effects of alcohol and fixation-task difficulty on choice reaction time to extrafoveal stimulation. *Quarterly Journal of Studies on Alcohol,* **34**, 89–103.

Hyde, J.S. (1984) How large are gender differences in aggression? A developmental meta-analysis. *Developmental Psychology,* **20**, 722–36.

Jessor, R.L., Collins, M.I. and Jessor, S.L. (1972) On becoming a drinker: Social-psychological aspects of an adolescent transition. *Annals of the New York Academy of Science,* **197**, 199–213.

Jessor, R. and Jessor, S.L. (1977) *Problem Behavior and Psychosocial Development – A Longitudinal Study of Youth*. New York: Academic Press.

Jessor, R., Jessor, S.L. and Finney, J. (1973) A social psychology of marijuana use: Longitudinal studies of high school and college youth. *Journal of Personality and Social Psychology,* **26**(1), 1–15.

Jones, M.C. (1968) Personality correlates and antecedents in drinking patterns in adult males. *Journal of Consulting and Clinical Psychology,* **32**, 2–12.

Jones, M.C. (1971) Personality correlates and practices of drinking in women. *Journal of Consulting and Clinical Psychology,* **36**, 61–9.

Kalin, R., McClelland, D.C. and Kahn, M. (1965) The effects of male social drinking on fantasy. *Journal of Personality and Social Psychology,* **5**, 441–52.

Kandel, D.B. (1975) Stages in adolescent involvement in drug use. *Science,* **190**, 912–14.

Kandel, D.B. (1978) Homophily, selection and socialization in adolescent friendships. *American Journal of Sociology,* **80**(2), 427–36.

Kandel, D.B. (1980) Drug and drinking behaviour among youth. *Annual Review of Sociology,* **6**, 235–85.

Kandel, D.B. (1982) Epidemiological and psychosocial perspectives on adolescent drug use. *Journal of the American Academy of Child Psychiatry,* **21**(4), 328–47.

Kaplan, H.B. (1980) *Deviant Behavior in Defense of Self.* New York: Academic Press.

Kastl, A.J. (1969) Changes in ego functioning under alcohol. *Quarterly Journal of Studies on Alcohol,* **30**, 371–83.

Lang, A.R., Goeckner, D.J., Adesso, V.J. and Marlatt, G.A. (1975) Effects of alcohol on aggression in male social drinkers. *Journal of Abnormal Psychology,* **84**, 508–18.

Larsen, K.S., Coleman, D., Forbes, J. and Johnson, R. (1972) Is the subject's personality or the experimental situation a better predictor of a subject's willingness to administer shock to a victim? *Journal of Personality and Social Psychology,* **22**, 287–95.

Lavelle, T., Hammersley, R. and Forsyth, A. (1993) Is the 'addictive' personality merely delinquency? *Addiction Research,* **1**, 27–37.

Leigh, G., Tong, J.E. and Campbell, J.A. (1975) Effects of ethanol and tobacco on divided attention. *Quarterly Journal of Studies on Alcohol,* **36**, 1233–9.

Maccoby, E.E. and Jacklin, C.N. (1974) *The Psychology of Sex Differences.* Stanford, CA: Stanford University Press.

Maccoby, E.E. and Jacklin, C.N. (1980) Sex differences in aggression: A rejoinder and reprise. *Child Development,* **51**, 964–80.

McCord, J. (1979) Some child-rearing antecedents of criminal behaviour in adult men. *Journal of Personality and Social Psychology,* **37**, 1477–86.

McCord, J. (1986) Instigation and insulation: How families affect antisocial aggression. In D. Olweus, J. Block and M. Radke-Yarrow (eds), *Development of Antisocial and Prosocial Behavior: Research, Theories, and Issues,* 343–57. New York: Academic Press.

McCord, W. and McCord, J. (1960) *Origins of Alcoholism*. Stanford, CA: Stanford University Press.

MacKay, J.R. (1961) Clinical observations on adolescent problem drinkers. *Quarterly Journal of Studies on Alcohol,* **22**, 124–34.

McKechnie, R., Cameron, D., Cameron, I. and Drewery, J. (1977) Teenage drinking in south-west Scotland. *British Journal of Addiction,* **72**, 287–95.

McMurran, M. and Hollin, C. (1993) *Young Offenders and Alcohol-related Crime.* Chichester: Wiley.

Marsh, A., Dobbs, J. and White, A. (1986) *Adolescent Drinking.* London: HMSO.

Marsh, P. and Kibby, K.F. (1992) *Drinking and Public Disorder.* London: The Portman Group.

Marsh, P., Rosser, E. and Harre, R. (1978) *The Rules of Disorder.* London: Routledge & Kegan Paul.

May, C. (1992) A burning issue? Adolescent alcohol use in Britain 1970–1991. *Alcohol and Alcoholism,* **27**(2), 109–15.

May, C. (1993) Resistance to peer group pressure: An inadequate basis for alcohol education. *Health Education Research,* **8**(2), 159–65.

Mayer, J.E. (1988) The personality characteristics of adolescents who use and misuse alcohol. *Adolescence,* **23**(90), 383–404.

Mayfield, D. (1976) Alcoholism, alcohol intoxication and assaultive behavior. *Diseases of the Nervous System* **37**, 228–91.

Mayfield, D. and Allen, D. (1967) Alcohol and effect: A psychopharmacological study. *American Journal of Psychiatry,* **123**, 1346–51.

MCM Research (1990) *Conflict and Violence in Pubs.* Oxford: MCM Research Ltd.

Milgram, S. (1974) *Obedience to Authority: An Experimental View.* New York: Harper & Row.

Miller, N.E. (1941) The frustration–aggression hypothesis. *Psychological Review,* **48**, 337–42.

Mills, K.C. and Ewing, J.A. (1977) The effect of low dose intravenous alcohol on human information processing. In M. Gross (ed.), *Advances in Experimental Medicine and Biology,* Vol. 85b: *Alcohol Intoxication and Withdrawal* 111b (Studies in Alcohol Dependence). New York: Plenum.

Moser, G. and Levy-Leboyer, C. (1985) Inadequate environment and situation control: Is a malfunctioning phone always an occasion for aggression? *Environment and Behaviour,* **17**, 520–33.

Mugford, S.K. (1994) Studies in the natural history of cocaine use – theoretical afterword. *Addiction Research,* **2**(1), 127–33.

Myers, T. (1982) Alcohol and violent crime re-examined: Self reports from two sub-groups of Scottish male prisoners. *British Journal of Addiction*, **77**, 399–413.

Newcomb, T. (1961) *The Acquaintance Process.* New York: Holt, Rinehart & Winston.

Newcomb, T. (1962) Student peer-group influence. In N. Sanford (ed.), *The American College: A Psychological and Social Interpretation of the Higher Learning.* New York: Wiley.

Newcomb, M.D. and Bentler, P.M. (1988) *Consequences of Adolescent Drug Use.* London: Sage Publications.

Newcomb, M.D. and McGee, L. (1989) Adolescent alcohol use and other delinquent behaviors: A one-year longitudinal analysis controlling for sensation seeking. *Criminal Justice and Behavior* **16**(3), 345–69.

O'Connor, J. (1978) *The Young Drinkers.* London: Tavistock Publications.

O'Doherty, F. (1988) The effect of naturally occurring life events on changes in consumption of alcohol, tobacco and heroin. PhD thesis, University of Strathclyde.

Oetting, E.R. and Beauvais, F. (1986) Peer cluster theory: Drugs and the adolescent. *Journal of Counseling and Development,* **65** (September), 17–22.

Oetting, E.R. and Beauvais, F. (1987) Peer cluster theory, socialization characteristics, and adolescent drug use: A path analysis. *Journal of Counseling Psychology,* **34**(2), 205–13.

Oliver, J.E. (1993) Intergenerational transmission of child abuse: rates, research, and clinical implications. *American Journal of Psychiatry,* **150**(9) (September), 1315–24.

Olweus, D. (1984) Aggressors and their victims: bullying at school. In N. Frude and H. Gault (eds), *Disruptive Behavior in Schools.* New York: Wiley.

Parker, E.S., Alkana, R.L., Birnbaum, I.M., Hartley, J.T. and Noble, E.P. (1974) Alcohol and the disruption of cognitive processes. *Archives of General Psychiatry,* **31**, 824–8.

Parker, H. (1993) Finding threads in the crime–alcohol tangle. In J.

Russell (ed.), *Alcohol and Crime: Proceedings of a Mental Health Foundation Conference*. London: Mental Health Foundation.

Pearce, J. (1992) What can be done about the bully? In M. Elliot (ed.), *Bullying: A Practical Guide to Coping for Schools.* Harlow: Longman.

Pearson, G. (1988) The roots of violence. *British Medical Journal,* **297**, 1352–3.

Pernanen, K. (1976) Alcohol and crimes of violence. In B. Kissin and H. Begleiter (eds), *The Biology of Alcoholism: Social Aspects of Alcoholism,* Vol. 4. New York: Plenum.

Plant, M.A. and Foster, J. (1991) Teenagers and alcohol: results of a Scottish national survey. *Drug and Alcohol Dependence,* **28**, 203–10.

Plant, M.A., Peck, D.F. and Samuel, E. (1985) *Alcohol, Drugs and School-leavers.* London: Tavistock Publications.

Plant, M.A., Peck, D.F. and Stuart, R. (1982) Self-reported drinking habits and alcohol related consequences among a cohort of Scottish teenagers. *British Journal of Addiction,* **77**, 75–90.

Pliner, P. and Cappell, H. (1974) Modification of affective consequences of alcohol: A comparison of social and solitary drinking. *Journal of Abnormal Psychology,* **83**, 418–25.

Ray, M.C. and Downs, W.R. (1986) An empirical test of labelling theory using longitudinal data. *Journal of Research in Crime and Delinquency,* **23**(2), 169–94.

Reinisch, J.M. and Sanders, S.A. (1986) A test of sex differences in aggressive response to hypothetical conflict situations. *Journal of Personality and Social Psychology,* **50**, 1045–9.

Reuband, K.H. (1977) The pathological and subcultural model of drug use: A test of two contrasting explanations. In J. Madden, R. Walker and W. Kenyon (eds), *Alcoholism and Drug Dependence*. New York: Plenum Press.

Ried, L.D. (1989) A path analytic examination of differential social control theory. *Journal of Drug Education,* **19**(2), 139–56.

Royal College of General Practitioners (1986) *Alcohol: a Balanced View*. London.

Royal College of Psychiatrists (1979) *Alcohol and Alcoholism.* London: Tavistock Publications.

Royal College of Psychiatrists (1986) *Alcohol: Our Favourite Drug.* London: Tavistock Publications.

Schachter, S. (1964) The interaction of cognitive and physiological determinants of emotional state. In L. Berkowitz (ed.), *Advances in Experimental Social Psychology,* Vol. 1, 49–80. New York: Academic Press.

Schachter, S. and Singer, J. (1962) Cognitive, social, and physiological determinants of emotional state. *Psychological Review,* **69**, 379–99.

Schaffer, R. (1977) *Mothering*. Glasgow: Fontana/Open Books, Collins.

Schroeder, D.S., Laflin, M.T. and Weis, D.L. (1993) Is there a relationship between self-esteem and drug use? Methodological and statistical limitations of the research. *Journal of Drug Issues* (Fall), 645–65.

Segal, B. (1986) Intervention and prevention of drug-taking behaviour. A need for divergent approaches. *The International Journal of the Addictions,* **21**(2), 165–73.

Shaffer, H.J. (1986) Observations on substance abuse theory. *Journal of Counseling and Development,* **65**, 26–8.

Sharpe, D. and Lowe, G. (1989) Adolescents and alcohol: A review of the recent British research. *Journal of Adolescence,* **12**, 295–307.

Skinner, B.F. (1959) *Cumulative Record*. New York: Appleton-Century-Crofts.

Smith, R.C., Parker, E.S. and Noble, E.P. (1975) Alcohol and effect in dyadic social interaction. *Psychosomatic Medicine,* **37**, 25–40.

Smyth, M. and Browne, F. (1992) *General Household Survey 1990.* London: HMSO.

Spielberger, C.D. (1983) *Manual for the State–Trait Anxiety Inventory.* Palo Alto, CA: Consulting Psychologists Press.

Spielberger, C.D. (1988) *State–Trait Anger Expression Inventory: Professional Manual.* Odessa, FL: PAR Inc.

Stacey, B. and Davies, J. (1970) Drinking behaviour in childhood and adolescence: An evaluative review. *British Journal of Addiction,* **65**, 203–12.

Stein, J.A., Newcomb, M.D. and Bentler, P.M. (1987) An 8-year study of multiple influences on drug use and drug use consequences. *Journal of Personality and Social Psychology,* **53**(6), 1094–105.

Taylor, S.P. (1967) Aggressive behaviour and physiological arousal as a function of provocation and the tendency to inhibit aggression. *Journal of Personality,* **35**, 297–310.

Taylor, S.P. and Gammon, C.B. (1975) Effects of type and dose of alcohol on human physical aggression. *Journal of Personality and Social Psychology,* **32**, 169–75.

Taylor, S.P. and Gammon, C.B. (1976) Aggressive behavior of intoxicated subjects: The effect of third party intervention. *Journal of Studies on Alcohol,* **37**, 917–30.

Taylor, S.P., Gammon, C.B. and Capasso, D.R. (1976) Aggression as a function of alcohol and threat. *Journal of Personality and Social Psychology,* **34**, 938–41.

Taylor, S.P. and Leonard, K.E. (1983) Alcohol and human physical aggression. In R.G. Green and R.I. Donnerstein (eds), *Aggression: Theoretical and Empirical Reviews,* Vol. 2. New York: Academic Press.

Thomas, A. and Chess, S. (1977) *Temperament and Development.* New York: Brunner/Mazel.

Thomas, M., Goddard, E., Hickman, M. and Hunter, P. (1994) *General Household Survey 1992.* London: HMSO.

Tinklenberg, J. (1973) Drugs and crime. In National Commission on Marijuana and Drug Abuse, *Drug Use in America: Problem in Perspective,* Appendix to Vol. 1, 242–99. Washington, DC: US Government Printing Office.

Tuck, M. (1989) *Drinking and Disorder: A Study of Non-Metropolitan Violence.* London: HMSO.

Tuck, M. (1993) Alcohol and crime – the British experience. In J. Russell (ed.), *Alcohol and Crime: Proceedings of a Mental Health Foundation Conference.* London: Mental Health Foundation.

Velleman, R. and Orford, J. (1993) The importance of family discord in explaining childhood problems in the children of problem drinkers. *Addiction Research,* **1**, 39–57.

Virkhunen, M. (1974) Alcohol as a factor precipitating aggression and conflict behaviour leading to homicide. *British Journal of Addiction,* **69**, 149–54.

Voss, H.L. and Hepburn, J.R. (1968) Patterns in criminal homicide in Chicago. *Journal of Criminal Law, Criminology and Police Science,* **59**, 499–508.

Walmsley, R. (1986) *Personal Violence*. Home Office Research Study No. 89. London: HMSO.

Walmsley, R. (1992) *The National Prison Survey 1991*. Home Office Research Study No. 128. London: HMSO.

West, D.J. (1982) *Delinquency: Its Roots, Careers and Prospects.* London: Heinemann.

White, H.R., Brick, J. and Hansell, S. (1992) *A Longitudinal Investigation of Alcohol Use and Aggression in Adolescence*. Proceedings of the International Conference on Alcohol and Aggression, New Jersey.

White, H.R., Johnson, V. and Horowitz, A. (1986) An application of three deviance theories to adolescent substance use. *The International Journal of the Addictions,* **21**(3), 347–66.

Williams, A. (1970) College problem drinkers: A personality profile. In G.L. Maddox (ed.), *The Domesticated Drug: Drinking Among Collegians.* New Haven, CT: College and University Press.

Wills, T.A. and Vaughan, R. (1989) Social support and substance use in early adolescence. *Journal of Behavioral Medicine,* **12**(4), 321–39.

Wilson, J.Q. and Herrnstein, R.J. (1985) *Crime and Human Nature*. New York: Simon & Schuster.

Wolff, S. (1985) Non-delinquent disturbance of conduct. In M. Rutter and L. Hersov (eds), *Child and Adolescent Psychiatry: Modern Approaches*. Oxford: Blackwell Scientific.

Wolfgang, M.E. and Strohm, R.B. (1956) The relationship between alcohol and criminal homicide. *Quarterly Journal of Studies on Alcohol,* **17**, 411–25.

Wolfgang, M.E., Thorberry, T.P. and Figlio, R.M. (1987) *From Boy to Man. From Delinquency to Crime.* Chicago: University of Chicago Press.

Wragg, J. (1992) *An Evaluation of a Model of Drug Education.* Monograph Series No. 22. Canberra: Australian Government Publishing Service.

Yancy, W.S., Nader, P.R. and Burnham, K. (1972) Drug use and attitudes of high school students. *Paediatrics,* **50**(5), 739–45.

Zucker, R.A. and Gomberg, E.S.L. (1986) Etiology of alcoholism reconsidered. *American Psychologist,* **41**, 783–93.

Zuckerman, M. and Como, P. (1983) Sensation seeking and arousal systems. *Personality and Individual Differences,* **4**(4), 381–6.

INDEX